# STANDARD SECURITIES CALCULATION METHODS

Fixed Income Securities Formulas
for
Price, Yield, and Accrued Interest

Volume I
Third Edition

By

Jan Mayle
President

Securities Industry Association

120 Broadway, New York, NY  10271-0080 • (212) 608-1500 • Fax: (212) 608-1604

ISBN 1-882936-01-9

Printed in the United States of America

# TABLE OF CONTENTS

# INTRODUCTION

This revision of the SIA Standard Securities Calculations Methods book was done at the request of and under the auspices of the Securities Industry Association. As with the original and the first revision, it contains formulas and discussions of calculating techniques for the computation of yields and prices for municipal, corporate, money market, US. Government and Federal Agency securities.

The Formulas presented here when used for municipals are in general agreement with those required by Rule G-33 of the Municipal Securities Rulemaking Board. Formulas for other securities are in agreement with generally accepted industry methods.

This book is an update of the 1986 revised edition. Formulas have been added to assist those responsible for price and yield computations on instruments with odd first and/or odd last coupon periods. A common thread runs throughout the calculations for all these securities. It is the basic formula which has been used for years to compute the present value of future money, Formula 7 (Formula 4 in previous editions). This formula has been expanded and shrunk for various types of securities. However, it is still the basic formula for our fixed income industry. Understanding Formula 7 and its basic principles will provide a foundation for understanding the modifications made in order to compute yields and prices on all types of securities.

The book is organized in three basic sections: instruments described by classification, calculation methods and formulas, and the appendices.

Descriptions for instruments have been compiled from and referenced against various sources and give basic information as to the nature and characteristics of various securities.

The methods of calculation and formulas are broken down as to: (1) General Considerations, (2) Day Counting, (3) Price-Yield Computations, (4) Concessions, (5) Iteration Theory and Solving for Yield, and (6) Estimated Yield.

"General Considerations" for calculations is a synopsis of associated data required for proper price-yield computations. "Day Counting" includes the method of computing the number of days between two dates based on the four generally accepted day count bases. The "Price-Yield Computations" section is subdivided into: (1) Discount, (2) Interest at Maturity, (3) "Regular" Periodic Interest Payments, (4) Odd First Coupons, (5) Odd Last Coupons, (6) Odd First and Last Coupons, (7) Zero Coupon, and (8) Stepped Coupons. "Iteration Theory and Solving for Yield" explains methods of repetitive calculation for the generation of a yield when given a dollar price for a periodic security. "Estimated Yield" gives a method for calculating a first guess of yield which is needed by any iterative method.

The Appendix contains: (1) copies of important rules to be considered when pricing securities (NASD Section 46, MSRB Rule G-33 and NSCC Concession Rule), and (2) several benchmarks for each formula, providing comparative calculations for user verification.

It is anticipated, as in the original book and the first revised edition, that there will be some unanswered questions and suggestions for improvements. The intention of the author is to present a compilation of formulas for the calculation of yields and prices for the current diversification of fixed income securities traded in our market.

Any reader having comments or suggestions should send them to the Securities Industry Association, 120 Broadway, 35th Floor, New York, NY 10271.

# ACKNOWLEDGEMENTS

This update has been made possible through the efforts of many individuals and organizations, to whom I am deeply grateful. The original volume resulted from a request by the Operations Committee of the Securities Industry Associations (SIA). The SIA's Operations Committee has, over the years, helped ensure that the calculations contained in this book are accurate and reflect recent product developments.

My thanks to the SIA's staff for their support, especially Tom Monahan, for shepherding the project from its initiation by the Operations Committee of the SIA; Rosalie Pepe for her untiring efforts in coordinating the proofreading and publishing of the present volume; and Ellen Fuchsman for her graphic design assistance.

I am also indebted to Gary Bronson, Professor in the Department of Information Systems and Sciences at Fairleigh Dickinson University and Richard Bronson, Professor in the Department of Mathematics and Computer Science at Fairleigh Dickinson University for their contributed article, which adds greatly to the value of this work.

The technical challenges in bringing this book to fruition were enormous. Much thanks to Charles Basner, Vice President of TIPS, Inc. and John J. Lynch Jr., Executive Vice President of J.F. Hartfield and 1992 chairman of SIA's Operations Committee for their proofing and reproofing efforts; and to R. Troy Keiper, TIPS, Inc. for page layout and formatting assistance.

And finally, thanks to the staff at TIPS, Inc. for their tireless efforts in the tedious, thankless job of double and triple checking the benchmark calculations.

Jan Mayle
TIPS, Inc.

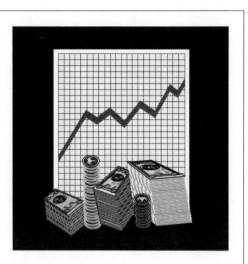

## TREASURY ISSUES:

### Treasury Certificates of Indebtedness

When offered, certificates of indebtedness are issued in bearer form only and have a fixed maturity, not exceeding one year from issue date. Interest is at a fixed rate. No unmatured certificates are presently outstanding.

### Treasury Bills

A Treasury Bill is an obligation of the United States Government to pay a fixed sum after a specified number of days from the date of issue. These debt instruments are sold by the Treasury at a discount through competitive bidding, and the return to the investor is the difference between the purchase price and the face, or par value. The discount rate on a Treasury bill of a given maturity is calculated using a 360-day year.

Such a rate of return cannot be compared directly with the yield to maturity of a coupon-bearing security, since yields to maturity on coupon issues are calculated by using another formula, and by using an actual-day instead of a 360-day year.

Treasury bills are issued in a variety of maturities and denominations, tailored to meet the needs of a diverse group of investors seeking both liquidity and income in a single investment. Bills are currently offered on a regular schedule with maturities of 91 days, 182 days, and 52 weeks. Treasury bills are issued only in book-entry form in accounts established at the Treasury and receipts are given as evidence of ownership.

### Treasury Notes

Notes of each series have a fixed maturity of not less than one nor more than ten years from date of issue, when the principal amount becomes payable. They bear interest at fixed rates, payable semi-annually. Since mid-1986, Treasury notes have been available only in book-entry form.

### Treasury Bonds

Bonds of each series have a fixed maturity, usually more than ten years from date of issue when the principal amount becomes payable. When so provided in the offering circulars, bonds may be called for redemption before maturity at the option of the United States, on and after specified dates, on four month's notice. Bonds bear interest at fixed rates, payable semi-annually. Interest payments and/or accrual ceases when the principal amount becomes payable whether at maturity or on an earlier date. Since mid-1986, Treasury bonds have been available only in book-entry form. Some series of outstanding bonds issued prior to 1966 are redeemable at par before call or maturity for the sole purpose of applying the entire proceeds to payment of the Federal estate tax on a deceased owner's estate.

### Treasury Strips

"STRIPS," available since 1985, are Treasury securities whose interest and principal payments have been divided into separate securities. It is the industry convention to calculate price and yield using semi-annual "quasi-coupon periods".

## FEDERAL AGENCY ISSUES:

Certain Federal Government corporations and agencies established by law to implement the Federal Government's various lending programs issue securities to finance their activities. Federal Land Banks, Federal Intermediate Credit Banks, Banks for Cooperatives, Federal Home Loan Banks, and the Federal National Mortgage Association (FNMA) constitute the major sources of agency securities. A number of other Federal agencies come to the market from time to time to offer their own debentures, to sell participations in their loan portfolios, or to sell some of their loans outright. These include the Tennessee Valley Authority, the Federal Housing Administration, etc. For a complete review and description of Federal agency issues and instruments, it is suggested that reference be made to The Public Securities Association's "Government Securities Manual."

The interest and principal of most Federal agency issues are guaranteed only by the issuing agency, not by the Federal Government. Such issues are sometimes referred to as "non guaranteed" debt. Exceptions include obligations of various agencies such as the Federal Housing Administration and the Farmers Home Administration which are directly guaranteed by the Federal Government.

Most agency securities bear a fixed rate of interest, and interest on the longer obligations is usually paid semi-annually. Exceptions include the Farmers Home Administration which pays interest only once a year, and three other agencies which pay only at maturity. The Tennessee Valley Authority, the Commodity Credit Corporation, and FNMA have sold short-term notes at a discount, where the interest is the difference between the discount price and par.

Maturity patterns vary widely among individual agencies. For instance, the Federal Intermediate Credit Banks and the Banks for Cooperatives usually sell six-to-nine-month paper, while the Federal Home Loan Banks, the Federal Land Banks, and FNMA offer both short-term and long-term securities.

Call features also vary; some agency issues are noncallable, while others are callable by the issuing agency after a specified period of time. Export-Import Bank notes offer the investor the option of reselling the notes to the agency under certain terms. Holders of Farmers Home Administration notes may extend the maturity of the notes or redeem them after the initial fixed

maturity of the Government's insurance endorsement has been reached.

Interest income and principal on most agency issues are subject to all Federal taxes but are usually exempt from all state and local taxes except inheritance and gift taxes. This is true of obligations of the Farmers Home Administration and any securities issued directly by FNMA.

A certificate of participation represents a beneficial interest in a pool of agency loans or mortgages. It is a formal credit instrument carrying a contractual interest obligation on a specified principal amount. In contrast to an outright sale of assets in which the title to the asset actually is transferred to the investor, the investor does not acquire title to any of the pooled assets at any time. Rather, the issuing agency continues to hold the pooled loans and to receive interest and principal payments on them. These payments, in turn, are used to service the certificates. The Commodity Credit Corporation initiated sales of Certificates of Participation in a pool of crop loans in 1953, and the Export-Import Bank began selling participation in its loan portfolio in 1962. But the first sale of certificates by FNMA in November 1964 probably marked their beginning as a significant new instrument of agency financing.

Under recent legislation passed by Congress, certificates of participation are, in effect, guaranteed. The Export-Import Bank and the Commodity Credit Corporation sell their own certificates. Those of a number of other agencies are sold under GNMA supervision and are serviced by a pool of loans of the several agencies. The law authorizes the selling agency to make "indefinite and unlimited" drawings on the Treasury, if needed, to service the certificates. Because of this provision, the Attorney General of the United States has designated all participation certificates as obligations of the United States.

## BC Debentures (CO-Ops)

The Banks for Cooperatives debentures are the joint obligations of the thirteen Banks for Cooperatives. The debentures are generally issued on a monthly basis. They are issued only in book-entry form with minimum denominations of $1,000. Their maturities range from six months to three years. Interest is payable at maturity or, in the case of longer term debentures, on a semi-annual basis. Interest is paid by any Bank for Cooperatives, Federal Reserve Bank, or the U. S. Treasury.

## Export-Import Bank (Ex-Im's)

The Export-Import Bank issues include participation certificates (PC's) and debentures. The participation certificates were issued in denominations ranging from $5,000 to $1 million and pay interest semi-annually. Debentures are issued in denominations as small as $5,000.

## FHDA Notes

The Farmers Home Administration (FHDA), an agency within the Department of Agriculture, extends real estate and housing loans to farmers and other rural residents. It then assembles those assets into blocks with face value of about $100,000, $500,000, or $1 million and sells "insurance contracts" covering the assets to private investors. Ownership of the contracts is registered with the Federal Reserve Bank of New York and denominational changes of the contracts are not permitted. They pay interest annually.

## FHLB

Federal Home Loan Bank (FHLB) issues bonds and discount notes to provide funds to the twelve regional Home Loan Banks for lending to member savings institutions. Bonds are issued in denominations ranging from $10,000 to $1 million, and pay interest semi-annually at any Federal Reserve Bank. Discount notes are issued in denominations from $100,000 to $1 million and payment at maturity is only at the New York Federal Reserve Bank. Both types of securities are issued in book-entry form only.

## FHA Debentures

The long-term debentures issued by the Federal Housing Administration (FHA) are rather specialized instruments that cannot be considered capital market instruments, although they are usually included in discussions of Federal Agency securities. They are not uniform in terms of maturity, yield, or denomination and, therefore, are not easily traded on a secondary market. They are issued as payment to a mortgagee who has purchased an FHA-insured mortgage that has gone into default. FHA acquires either the mortgage or the property from the mortgagee and, in return, issues a debenture with face value, maturity, and yield identical to those of the mortgage contract. The mortgagee can then either hold the debenture until it matures, sell it to another investor, or use it for repayment of FHA insurance premiums. FHA will accept the debentures at face value from holders of insured mortgages for payment of FHA insurance premiums. Thus, the holders are principally mortgage lenders who acquired the debentures when some of their mortgages went into default or purchased them for use in paying FHA insurance premiums.

## FICB Debentures

The Federal Intermediate Credit Banks (FICB) debentures are the joint obligations of the twelve district Federal Intermediate Credit Banks. The debentures are issued on a monthly basis in book-entry form only. Their maturities range up to five years with minimum denominations of $5,000. Interest is payable at maturity, or in the case of longer term debentures, on a semi-annual basis. Interest is paid by any Federal Intermediate Credit Bank, Federal Reserve Bank, or the U.S. Treasury. New Issues are available in book-entry form only.

### FLB Bonds

The Federal Land Bank (FLB) bonds are the joint obligations of the twelve Federal Land Banks. The bonds are issued in book-entry form only in denominations that range from $1,000 to $100,000 and normally are not callable. Interest on the bonds is paid semi-annually by any Federal Land Bank, Federal Reserve Bank, or the U.S. Treasury

### FNMA Debentures (Fannie Mae's)

The Federal National Mortgage Association (FNMA) debentures are direct obligations of the Association and are issued to finance its secondary market operations in Government-insured or guaranteed home mortgages. The fixed rate debentures are issued in denominations ranging from $10,000 to $500,000, are not callable, and pay interest semi-annually at any Federal Reserve Bank or at the Treasury Department. These debentures are issued in book-entry form only.

### FNMA Notes

The Federal National Mortgage Association also issues short-term notes similar to commercial paper. These are sold at published rates with maturity ranges from 30 to 360 days.

### GNMA PC's (Ginnie Mae's)

In 1964, FNMA became the trustee of three trusts made up of debt obligations owned by FNMA, the Veterans Administration, and other agencies within the Federal Government. FNMA then issued participation certificates (PC's), which are bond-type instruments giving the owners a beneficial interest in the trusts. These and other forms of mortgage and asset-backed securities are not covered in this book. For informa-

tion on applicable calculation standards refer to the Public Securities Association's "Standard Formulas for the Analysis of Mortgage Backed and Other Related Securities".

### U.S. Postal Service Bonds

The U.S. Postal Service made its first public debt offering in January 1972, when it sold $250 million of 6 7/8 percent 25-year bonds. The bonds are callable in ten years, are not guaranteed by the Federal Government, and are exempted from state and local income and property taxes. They are issued with minimum denominations of $10,000 with interest payable semi-annually.

### TVA Bonds

The Tennessee Valley Authority (TVA) has issued 25-year power bonds since 1959 when Congress authorized the utility to issue bonds and notes. They are issued in multiples of $5,000 and are callable, usually after five or ten years. In most respects, these bonds are more similar to private utility bonds than to Federal Agency issues. Interest is payable on a semi-annual basis.

## STATE AND LOCAL GOVERNMENT ISSUES:

### Municipal Bonds

States, state agencies, local governments within states, and public authorities periodically issue debt obligations called municipal bonds. Proceeds from these bond issues are used for various purposes such as construction of buildings, numerous public programs, and general needs of the issuing unit. The interest received from such securities is considered exempt from Federal income taxes and are generally exempt from state and local income taxes in the state in which the securities are issued.

The security pledged to the payment of bond principal and interest differentiate municipal bonds. When the pledge of the borrower is the full faith and credit of the issuing unit, bonds are backed by all of the borrower's resources and secured by taxes collectible on all taxable property within the borrower's jurisdiction, usually without limitation of rate or amount. These bonds are referred to as "general obligation" bonds. Other classifications include "Revenue" and "Assessment" categories under which variations of the security and payment liabilities exist (such as limited tax, lease obligations, etc.)

Municipal bonds are obtainable in registered or book entry form. Most issues are denominated in $5,000 bonds. Interest is payable generally on a semi-annual basis.

Although municipal bonds are sometimes issued as term bonds, the majority are issued as serial bonds. Certain issues combine both term and serial maturities.

Some bonds of a given issue, prior to maturity, may be redeemable depending upon the provisions of the call features of the issue.

### Short-term Tax Exempt Notes

Various public bodies issue short-term tax exempt obligations referred to as "tax exempt notes." They are exempt from Federal income taxes and are available in registered or book entry form in minimum denominations of $1,000. Maturities usually extend from thirty days to one year with accrued (coupon) interest payable generally at maturity. Some notes are issued with periodic coupons.

There are many types of short-term notes available: Project Notes (PN's); Bond Anticipation Notes (BAN's); Tax Anticipation Notes (TAN's); etc. Additionally, tax anticipation warrants are available.

## CORPORATE ISSUES:

### Corporate Bonds

A Corporate Bond is debt issued by a corporation which usually pays interest periodically and the principal at redemption. Most have call provisions which allow the issuing corporation to redeem the bonds before their stated maturity. Some different types of corporate bonds are:

Coupon Bonds pay interest at a specified rate every period until redemption at which time the par value is paid.

A Zero Coupon Bond has an interest rate of zero percent. It is issued at a large discount from par but, it is treated as a periodic payment security not a discount security. This means that its price and yield are calculated using present value theory with semi-annual quasi-coupon periods rather than on a simple interest basis.

Payment-in-Kind (PIK) Bonds in their simplest form pay interest periodically at a specified interest rate as additional bonds rather than as cash. In another form they pay interest as additional bonds for a specified period of time then switch to paying interest as cash. In a third form they pay part of the periodic interest as additional bonds and part as cash.

Convertible Bonds in addition to paying interest give the bond holder the option of converting the bond into stock on or after some specified date at a specified price.

Floating Rate Bonds pay interest based on an rate which changes (floats) over time. The interest rate is generally tied to some industry quoted interest rate such as the prime rate or LIBOR.

### Medium Term Notes

Medium Term Note is another name for a corporate bond which has a maturity of less than ten years. It was the first type of corporate debt to have odd last coupon periods and therefor is sometimes incorrectly considered a different type of security than a corporate bond.

### Commercial Paper

Commercial Paper technically includes all short-term evidences of indebtedness of business firms, that is, promissory notes of business firms, commercial drafts, domestic acceptances, and open market commercial paper. However, in the money market, commercial paper is generally defined as unsecured short-term notes issued in bearer form by large, well-known businesses.

This type of money market paper has several unique and identifying characteristics. For example, maturities on commercial paper range from a few days to nine months (270 days). Notes with a maturity of more than 270 days are uncommon because such issues must be registered with the Securities and Exchange Commission. In general, maturity dates on individual issues reflect the needs of either the buyer or the issuer, as well as market conditions.

Commercial Paper is commonly issued in multiples of $5,000, although million-dollar notes are not uncommon. The exact denomination is always arranged to suit the convenience of the buyer.

There are basically two types of commercial paper: (1) direct paper; and (2) dealer paper. Directly placed paper is sometimes called "finance company paper" because the issuing companies are usually finance companies that sell their notes to investors without using the services of a dealer. The dealer paper market is composed of dealers who purchase notes outright from issuers. Commercial Paper dealers then generally place their paper with investors.

## OTHER INSTRUMENTS:

### Bankers' Acceptances

Bankers' Acceptances represent one type of a broad class of credit instruments known as bills of exchange. Bills of exchange, in turn, are drafts, or orders to pay specified amounts at a specified time, drawn on individuals, business firms, or financial institutions. When the drawee formally acknowledges his obligation to honor such a draft (usually by writing "Accepted" or " I Accept" with the appropriate signature across the face of the draft), it becomes an "acceptance." An acceptance which represents the liability of a well-known bank is, for obvious reasons, a more desirable credit instrument than one drawn on a little-known firm or individual. Maximum maturities are six months. Interest is calculated on a 360-day discount basis similar to Treasury Bills.

### Certificates of Deposit

A negotiable Certificate of Deposit, or CD, is a marketable receipt for funds deposited in a bank for a specified period at a specified rate of interest. Interest accruing CD's are payable either at maturity or periodically. CD's can also be issued on a discount basis.

The owner of the CD at the time of its maturity receives both principal and interest, while its readily salable feature enables the purchaser to retrieve his funds before maturity by selling the instrument to another holder.

CD's may be in registered or bearer form, although the latter is more convenient for secondary market trading. Denominations range from $100,000 to $10 million, depending on the size of the issuing bank and the type of CD customer it is trying to attract. Large New York banks seldom issue a CD of less than one million dollars.

**CMO's and Asset Backed Securities**

CMO's and Asset Backed Securities are a class of securities which are backed by collateral. The collateral can be anything from GNMAs and other mortgage-backed securities to auto loans and credit card debt. The interest and principal received on the collateral is divided up by the rules of the security and passed to the individual tranches.

To properly calculate price, yield, discount, and interest the following considerations need to be made.

1. The formula which applies to the particular security under consideration must be identified

2. The **day count basis** for the security must be determined and the number of days between the pertinent dates must be calculated.

3. **Industry rules** must be complied with (e.g. MSRB Rule G-33).

4. **Industry conventions** must be understood.

   In corporate and municipal bond pricing odd first and last coupon periods are ignored in calculating yield. However, in the corporate bond market there is a trend toward taking into account the odd coupon.

   The call price used in the formulas for zero coupon securities must be calculated from the Capital Accreted Value (CAV).

5. **Concessions** must be properly computed and applied to the price (or yield) to arrive at the actual cost of the security.

6. **Callable bond** calculations should take into consideration all call dates and call prices. The long established principle of a minimum assured yield to the purchaser should be followed.

7. **Accuracy of intermediate values** for all price, yield and interest calculations should be carried to at least ten significant decimals. When computing call price for zero coupon calculations, the CAV should be to at least ten significant decimals then multiplied by the percent and (a) truncated to three places for corporate and municipal bonds, and (b) rounded to three places for U.S. Treasuries and Federal Agency securities.

8. **Dollar price accuracy** of calculations for securities are as follows:

   a. For municipal and corporate securities, dollar prices should be accurate to seven places after the decimal, truncating to three decimals (truncating is to take place just prior to the display of price and calculation of principal).

   Examples: 99.987654 = 99.987

   b. For all other securities, with the exception of treasury bills, dollar price accuracy should be to seven places after the decimal, rounding to six decimals (rounding is to take place just prior to the display of price and calculation of principal).

   Examples: 99.9876546 = 99.987655

   c. For Treasury Bills, dollar price accuracy should be to eight places after the decimal, rounding to seven decimals (rounding is to take place just prior to the display of price and calculation of principal).

   Examples: 99.98765463 = 99.9876546

9. **Calculations for yield** should be at a minimum accurate to four places after the decimal point, rounding to three decimals (rounding is to take place just prior to display of yield).

   Examples:  4.6245% = 4.625%
   and  4.6244% = 4.624%

10. **No interest** is accrued in the formulas if the settlement date falls on an interest payment date; (i.e. if the maturity date is 7/5/99 and the settlement date is 1/5/93 for a semi-annual periodic payment security, then accrued days (A) equals 0 and days from settlement to next coupon (DSC) equals 181 days for the Actual/Actual or 180 days for the 30/360 day count basis).

Day Count Basis indicates the method in which the days in a month and the days in a year are to be counted. The notation used to identify Day Count Basis is (days in month)/(days in year). There are two fundamental Day Count Bases currently in use for U.S. domestic securities: 30/360 and Actual/Actual.

30/360: The first method considers the year (for example, the time from 1-1-93 to 1-1-93) to consist of twelve months of an equal length of 30 days each. Thus, a year has 360 days (12 x 30). This day count basis is identified by "30/360," meaning 30 days per month/360 days per year.

Actual/Actual: The second method treats each month as having the number of days that are actually in the month. Thus, the actual number of days are counted and the actual number of days per year are used. This day count basis is identified by "Actual/Actual," meaning actual number of days per month/actual number of days per year.

It is important to note that for short-term securities we use a combination of these two basic methods. This variation is based on the actual number of days between dates (numerator), and a year basis (denominator) of 360 days (Actual/360).

In this book, the term "days in year" or year basis is only used to calculate the value of the variables "B" and "E."

## DAY COUNT BASIS: 30/360

Months are considered to have 30 days each and the days between two dates is computed based on this. The time periods for which these rules may be used are listed below. For any other time periods see the note below.

| Time Period | From Date | To Date | Variable |
| --- | --- | --- | --- |
| days accrued | issue/dated | settlement | A |
| | prior coupon | settlement | A |
| days issued for | issue/dated | redemption | DIR |
| days in an odd first period | issue/dated | first coupon | DFC |
| | issue/dated | first quasi-coupon | DFC |
| days in an odd last period | last coupon | redemption | DLC |
| | last quasi-coupon | redemption | DLC |

To calculate the number of days between two dates (listed above), use the following variables and formulas.

$M1$ = month of the earlier date $\qquad$ $M2$ = month of the later date
$D1$ = day of the earlier date $\qquad$ $D2$ = day of the later date
$Y1$ = year of the earlier date $\qquad$ $Y2$ = year of the later date

Since all months can have only 30 days, we must adjust for the months that do not actually have 30 days before we can calculate the number of days between the two dates. This is accomplished by applying the following rules:

if $D2$ is the last day of February (28 in a non leap year; 29 in a leap year)
and $D1$ is the last day of February,
    change $D2$ to 30

if $D1$ is the last day of February,
    change $D1$ to 30

if $D2$ is 31 and $D1$ is 30 or 31,
    change $D2$ to 30

if $D1$ is 31,
    change $D1$ to 30

Now we can calculate the number of days between the two dates using the formula:

$$\text{Number of days} = (Y2 - Y1) * 360 + (M2 - M1) * 30 + (D2 - D1)$$

NOTE: To calculate the number of days in a time period other than those listed above the following rules should be applied:

The number of days in a year is always 360.
The number of days in a period is always 360 divided by the number of periods per year.
The number of days remaining in a period is always the number of days in the period minus the number of days accrued.

# EXAMPLE

The following example illustrates the calculation of the number of days between two dates using a 30/360 day count method.

| Prior coupon date | 01/31/1992 |
|---|---|
| Settlement date | 03/16/1992 |

$$M1 = 1$$
$$D1 = 31$$
$$Y1 = 1992$$
$$M2 = 3$$
$$D2 = 16$$
$$Y2 = 1992$$

D2 is not 31 so do not change it
if D1 = 31 then D1 = 30
D1 is 31, so change it to 30

$$D1 = 30$$

$$\text{Number of days} = (Y2 - Y1) * 360 + (M2 - M1) * 30 + (D2 - D1)$$

$$= (1985 - 1985) * 360 + (3 - 1) * 30 + (16 - 30)$$

$$= (0) * 360 + (2) * 30 + (-14)$$

$$= 0 + 60 - 14$$

$$= 46$$

DAY COUNT BASIS: Actual/Actual

For this day count basis the number of days between two dates is the actual number of calendar days. In order to calculate the actual number of days between two dates, you must first convert each date to a date offset (a number of days since a given base date). There are many methods to do this. Two of them are described below:

A. **Julian date method.** Many computer systems have a way to change a Gregorian date (MM/DD/YYYY) to a Julian date (number of days since some base date). If you have such a mechanism available to you, check that it is accurate and use it.

If you do not have a Julian date routine available to you, you can use the following formula. All of the calculations in this formula are integer arithmetic (the fractional part of all division steps is discarded before continuing).

M = month of year

D = day of month

Y = year

Julian = D - 32075 + (1461 * (Y + 4800 + (M - 14) / 12)) / 4

Julian = Julian + (367 * (M - 2 - ((M - 14) / 12) * 12)) / 12

Julian = Julian - (3 * ((Y + 4900 + (M - 14) / 12) / 100)) / 4

B. **Number of days since base date 00/00/0000 method.** This is quicker than the Julian date method. It requires a function that truncates a number (that is, discards the fractional part). We will call this the *integer* function.

M = month of year

D = day of year

Y = year

If M is less than or equal to 2 then

MP = 0 and YP = Y - 1

If M is greater than 2 then

MP = *integer* (0.4 * M + 2.3) and YP = Y

T = *integer* (YP / 4) - *integer* (YP / 100) + *integer* (YP / 400)

Days since base date = 365 * Y + 31 * (M - 1) + D + T - MP

Once you have converted both dates to date offsets subtract the earlier date from the later date to get the number of days between the two dates.

Number of days = Date offset ( later date ) - Date offset ( earlier date )

The following example illustrates the calculation of the number of days between two dates using an Actual/Actual day count method.

| | |
|---|---|
| First date | 01/31/1990 |
| Second date | 03/16/1991 |

The Date Offset of the first date = 21265
The Date Offset of the second date = 21674

Number of days = 21674 - 21625
= 409

DAY COUNT BASIS: Actual/360

Though the annual or year basis is 360 days, the counting method for the variables "DSC", "DIM", "A", etc. is done on the month basis of actual days.

For example:

1 January 1993 to 1 April 1993 is 90 days
1 January 1992 to 1 April 1992 is 91 days

It should be noted that in the second example 29 February 1992 was counted as a day.

DAY COUNT BASIS: Actual/365

The annual or year basis is 365 days, and does not consider the extra day in a leap year. Although the year basis is 365, the counting method for the variables "DSC", "DIM", "A", etc. is done on the month basis of actual days, including leap year. It is possible to have a fraction of 366/365.

Additional examples of the number of days between two dates.

|  |  | Actual/Actual | 30/360 |
|---|---|---|---|
| 01/01/93 to 02/21/93 | = | 51 days | 50 days |
| 02/01/93 to 03/01/93 | = | 28 days | 30 days |
| 02/01/92 to 03/01/92 | = | 29 days | 30 days |
| 01/01/93 to 01/01/94 | = | 365 days | 360 days |
| 01/15/93 to 02/01/93 | = | 17 days | 16 days |
| 02/15/93 to 04/01/93 | = | 45 days | 46 days |
| 03/31/93 to 04/30/93 | = | 30 days | 30 days |
| 03/31/93 to 12/31/93 | = | 275 days | 270 days |
| 03/15/93 to 06/15/93 | = | 92 days | 90 days |
| 11/01/93 to 03/01/94 | = | 120 days | 120 days |
| 12/31/93 to 02/01/94 | = | 32 days | 31 days |
| 07/15/93 to 09/15/93 | = | 62 days | 60 days |
| 08/21/93 to 04/11/94 | = | 233 days | 230 days |
| 03/31/93 to 04/01/93 | = | 1 day | 1 day |
| 12/15/93 to 12/31/93 | = | 16 days | 16 days |
| 12/15/93 to 12/30/93 | = | 15 days | 15 days |

$$\left[\sum_{i=1}^{NC} \frac{A_i}{NL_i}\right] * \left(\frac{R}{M}\right)$$

# INTEREST FORMULAS

Interest payments on all interest accruing or coupon bearing securities are calculated using the following formulas and are based on "simple interest" rather than "compound interest" principles.

| Formula Number | Description |
|---|---|
| A | Standard Interest Formula |
| B | Short Coupon Formula |
| C | Long Coupon Formula |

# DISCOUNT FORMULA

Sometimes, rather than earning interest, a security is sold at a discount and the discount amount represents the money earned on the instrument. The discount amount is equal to the difference between the par value and the principal or total amount invested. This, like interest in the above formulas, is computed based on "simple interest" rather than "compound interest" principles.

| Formula Number | Description |
|---|---|
| D | Discount Amount Formula |

# FORMULA A

## Standard Interest Formula

Calculation of accrued interest for securities with standard coupons (semi-annual, annual, etc.) or interest at maturity.

$$\text{Accrued Interest} = P * \frac{R}{M} * \frac{A}{D}$$

where:

A = Number of accrued days counted according to the day count basis. For periodic items, number of days from beginning of period to settlement date is used; for interest at maturity items, number of days from issue date to settlement date is used to calculate accrued interest, and number of days from issue date to maturity date is used to calculate the interest at maturity

D = For periodic items, number of days in interest or coupon period (represented by "E" in applicable price/yield formulas); for interest at maturity items, annual year basis (represented by "B" in applicable price/yield formulas)

M = Number of interest or coupon periods per year (M is equal to 1 for interest at maturity items)

P = Par Value (principal amount to be paid at maturity)

R = Annual interest or coupon rate as a decimal

## CORPORATE BOND

| | |
|---|---|
| Day Count Basis | 30/360 |
| Issue Date | 04/01/92 |
| First Interest Date | 10/01/92 |
| Settlement Date | 08/18/92 |

M = 2 → semi-annual coupon payments

D = 180 → since day count basis is 30/360 and the number of coupons per year is 2. (360 / 2 = 180)

P = $1000

R = 0.05 → interest/coupon rate of 5.00%

A = 137 → accrued days are found by determining the number of days from the prior coupon date (in this case, the issue date) to settlement date (04/01/92 to 08/18/92).

Thus:

$$\text{Accrued Interest} = 1000 * \frac{0.05}{2} * \frac{137}{180}$$

$$\text{Accrued Interest} = \$19.03$$

# FORMULA B

### Short Coupon Formula

To determine the accrued interest in a short coupon period, that coupon period's length must be adjusted to represent a normal length (NL) or quasi-coupon* period (NL replaces D in the standard formula).  This is done in one of the two following ways; *Odd first coupon:* by working backwards in time from the short coupon's interest payment date (first coupon date) to a date representing the first day of the quasi coupon period; *Odd last coupon:* by working forward in time from the short coupon's interest payment date (last coupon date before redemption) to a date representing the last day of the quasi coupon period.   This is only significant if the year basis is actual/actual.  The 30/360 year basis always has an equal length coupon period of 360 divided by the number of coupons normal per year.  The accrued interest is then calculated from the standard interest formula.

$$\text{Accrued Interest} = P * \frac{R}{M} * \frac{A}{NL}$$

where:

A  =  Accrued days

M  =  Number of coupon periods per year

NL  =  Number of days representing the quasi-coupon period

P  =  Par Value (principal amount to be paid at maturity)

R  =  Annual coupon rate as a decimal

---

* The term "quasi-coupon period" is used to represent the length of the coupon period that is standard for the security (semi-annual, annual, etc.).  Thus, a semi-annual corporate bond with three months for its first coupon period has one quasi-coupon period of 180 days.

### MUNICIPAL BOND

| | |
|---|---|
| Day Count Basis | 30/360 |
| Issue Date | 07/01/92 |
| First Interest Date | 10/01/92 |
| Settlement Date | 08/18/92 |

$M$ = 2 → semi-annual coupon payments

$NL$ = 180 → since day count basis is 30/360 and the number of coupons per year is 2. (360 / 2 = 180)

$P$ = $1000

$R$ = 0.05 → interest/coupon rate of 5.00%

$A$ = 47 → accrued days are found by determining the number of days from issue date to settlement date (07/01/92 to 08/18/92).

Thus:

$$\text{Accrued Interest} = 1000 * \frac{0.05}{2} * \frac{47}{180}$$

$$\text{Accrued Interest} = \$6.53$$

# FORMULA C

## Long Coupon Formula

To determine the accrued interest for long coupon periods, the number (NC) of quasi-coupon* periods must be calculated. This is done in one of the two following ways; *Odd long first coupon:* by working backwards in time from the long coupon's interest payment date (first coupon date) and adding together the number of standard coupon periods that would fit in the long coupon, rounding up to the next whole number; *Odd long last coupon:* by working forward in time from the long coupon's interest payment date (last coupon date before redemption) and adding together the number of standard coupon periods that would fit in the long coupon, rounding up to the next whole number. For example, between the issue date of 07/01/92 and the first coupon date of 04/01/93 there are 1½ six month periods or 2 (NC = 2) quasi-coupon periods.

$$\text{Accrued Interest} = P * \left(\frac{R}{M}\right) * \left[\sum_{i=1}^{NC} \frac{A_i}{NL_i}\right]$$

where:

$A_i$ = Number of accrued days for the ith quasi-coupon period within odd period

$M$ = Number of coupon periods per year

$NC$ = Number of quasi-coupon periods that fit in odd period. If this number contains a fractional part, raise it to the next whole number

$NL_i$ = Normal length in days of the ith quasi-coupon period within odd period

$P$ = Par Value (principal amount to be paid at maturity)

$R$ = Annual interest rate as a decimal

---

* The term "quasi-coupon period" is used to represent the length of the coupon period that is standard for the security (semi-annual, annual, etc.). Thus, a semi-annual municipal bond with nine months for its first coupon period has two quasi-coupon periods, each with a length of 180 days.

### TREASURY SECURITY

| Day Count Basis | Actual/Actual |
|---|---|
| Issue Date | 07/01/92 |
| First Interest Date | 04/01/93 |
| Settlement Date | 02/01/93 |

$M$ = 2

$A_1$ = 123    (10/01/92 - 02/01/93)

$A_2$ = 92    (07/01/92 - 10/01/92)

$NC$ = 2    (10/01/92 - 04/01/93)
            (04/01/92 - 10/01/92)

$NL_1$ = 182    (10/01/92 - 04/01/93)

$NL_2$ = 183    (04/01/92 - 10/01/92)

$P$ = \$10,000

$R$ = 0.075    (7½%)

Thus:

$$\text{Accrued Interest} = 10000 * \frac{0.075}{2} * \left(\frac{123}{182} + \frac{92}{183}\right)$$

$$= 10000 * 0.0375 * (0.675824 + 0.502732)$$

$$= 10000 * 0.0375 * 1.178556$$

$$= \$441.96$$

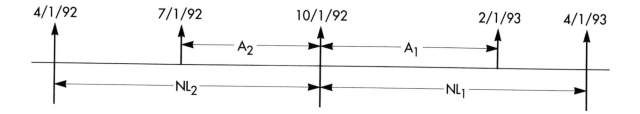

# FORMULA D

## Discount Formula

The discount amount can be found, if the price is known, using the following formula:

$$\text{Discount Amount} = (\text{Par Value}) - \left[(\text{Par Value}) * \text{Price}\right]$$

where:

| | | |
|---|---|---|
| Discount Amount | = | Difference between cost value and maturity value |
| Par Value | = | Par Value of the security (maturity value) |
| Price | = | Quoted price of the security divided by 100 |

The discount amount can be found, if the discount rate is known, by using the following discount formula:

$$\text{Discount Amount} = (\text{Par Value}) * DR * \frac{DSM}{B}$$

where:

| | | |
|---|---|---|
| B | = | Number of days in year (annual basis from day count basis) |
| DR | = | Discount Rate (as a decimal) |
| DSM | = | Number of days from settlement date to maturity date |

**TREASURY BILL**

| | |
|---|---|
| Par Value | $1,000 |
| Day Count Basis | Actual/360 |
| Settlement Date | 02/01/93 |
| Maturity Date | 06/15/93 |

$$DR = 0.065 \rightarrow \text{discount rate of } 6\tfrac{1}{2}\%$$

$$B = 360$$

$$DSM = 134 \quad (02/1/93 - 06/15/93)$$

$$\text{Discount Amount} = 1000 * 0.065 * \frac{134}{360}$$

$$= 1000 * 0.065 * 0.372222$$

$$= \$24.14$$

$$\frac{RV}{\left(1 + \dfrac{Y}{M}\right)^{N}}$$

**Please note:** *Formulas in this section for the calculation of price and yield which also appear in the 1986 Revised Edition of this book no longer have the same Formula Numbers.*

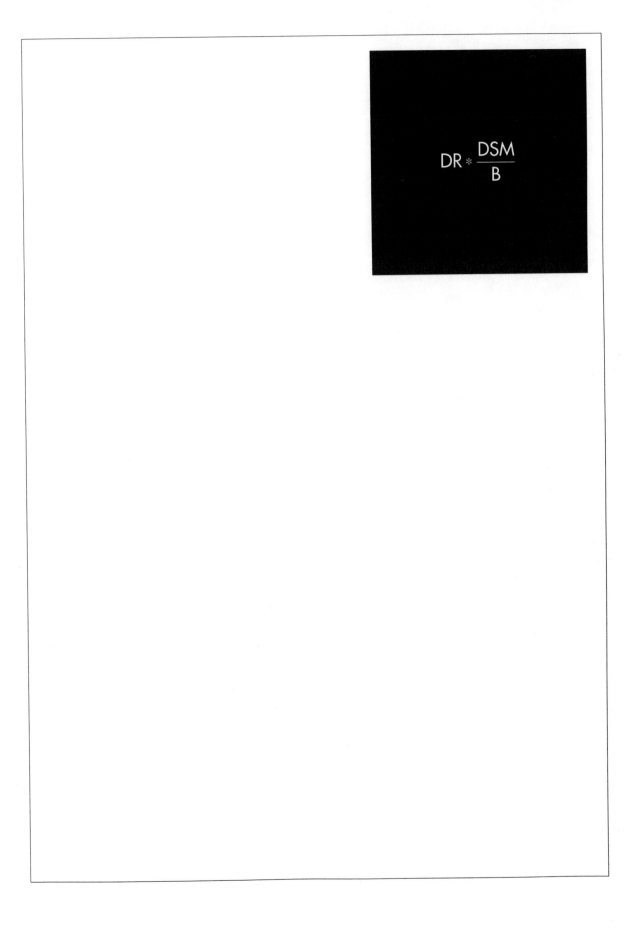

$$DR * \frac{DSM}{B}$$

## CALCULATIONS FOR DISCOUNTED SECURITIES

The following formulas are used with the traditional short term discounted securities such as Treasury Bills, Commercial Paper and Bankers Acceptances.  Unlike the "discount" calculations for Capital Accretion securities (see the section "Zero Coupon"), these formulas are based on simple interest and do not take compounding into account.

Two formulas are presented for calculating the price or yield of discount securities.  These formulas are:

| Formula Number | Description |
| --- | --- |
| 1 | Yield (given price) |
| 2 | Price (given discount rate) |

# FORMULA 1

[Yield (given price)]

$$Y = \left[\frac{RV - P}{P}\right] * \left[\frac{B}{DSM}\right]$$

B = Number of days in a year (annual basis)

DSM = Number of days from settlement date to maturity date

P = Dollar price per $100 par value

RV = Redemption value per $100 par value

Y = Annual Yield on investment with security held to maturity (as a decimal)*

NOTE: The first term calculates yield on invested dollars. The second term converts this yield to a per annum basis.

---

*The Annual Yield is not a coupon equivalent or bond equivalent yield, but rather a reflection of the simple interest return on an investment. It is sometimes referred to as the "money market yield."

# EXAMPLE

## BANKER'S ACCEPTANCE

The following example illustrates the calculation of the yield based on a given dollar price for a Banker's Acceptance.

| | | |
|---|---|---|
| Settlement Date | 02/07/93 | |
| Maturity Date | 06/06/93 | |
| Day Count Basis | Actual/360 | |
| B = 360 | | |
| DSM = 119 | (02/07/93 - 06/06/93) | |
| P = 97.975347 | | |
| RV = 100 | | |
| Y = 0.06251573 | | |
| Yield = 6.252% | | |

NOTE: Banker's Acceptances are not sold on a yield basis, but only at a discount rate. This example is provided for the purpose of showing how yield (as a rate of return on money invested) is calculated. The formula for discount rate is:

$$DR = \left[1 - \frac{P}{RV}\right] * \left[\frac{B}{DSM}\right]$$

Using the example above, DR = 6.125

# FORMULA 2

[Price (given discount rate)]

$$P = [RV] - \left[ DR * RV * \frac{DSM}{B} \right]$$

B  =  Number of days in a year (annual basis)

DR  =  Discount rate (as a decimal)

DSM  =  Number of days from settlement date to maturity date

P  =  Dollar price per $100 par value

RV  =  Redemption value per $100 par value

NOTE:  The first term is the redemption value.  The second term calculates the discount amount.

# EXAMPLE

## U.S. TREASURY BILL

The following example illustrates the calculation of the dollar price for a U.S. Treasury Bill given a discount rate.

| | | |
|---|---|---|
| Settlement Date | 02/07/92 | |
| Maturity Date | 03/01/92 | |
| Day Count Basis | Actual/360 | |
| B = | 360 | |
| DR = | 0.0535 | (5.35%) |
| DSM = | 23 | (02/07/92 to 03/01/92) |
| RV = | 100 | |
| P = | 99.6581944 | |
| Dollar Price = | 99.6581944 | |

$$\dfrac{1 + \dfrac{DIM}{B} * R}{1 + \dfrac{DSM}{B} * Y}$$

## CALCULATIONS FOR INTEREST AT MATURITY SECURITIES

Securities requiring interest at maturity calculations are those which do not have periodic interest payments, but rather one interest payment made at the maturity of the security. Certificates of Deposit and Interest Bearing Commercial Paper are examples of this type of security. The two formulas presented on the following pages allow for yield calculation (when given price) and price calculation (when given yield).

Interest at Maturity formulas differ from Interest Multiplier formulas (see page 105) in that the former are based on simple interest theory, while the latter are based on compound interest theory.

The Interest at Maturity formulas presented are:

| Formula Number | Description |
|---|---|
| 3 | Yield (given price) |
| 4 | Price (given yield) |

# FORMULA 3

[Yield (given price)]

$$Y = \left[ \dfrac{\left(1 + \left(\dfrac{DIM}{B} * R\right)\right) - \left(\dfrac{P}{100} + \left(\dfrac{A}{B} * R\right)\right)}{\dfrac{P}{100} + \left(\dfrac{A}{B} * R\right)} \right] * \dfrac{B}{DSM}$$

A   =   Number of days from issue date to settlement date (accrued days)

B   =   Number of days in a year (annual basis)

DIM   =   Number of days from issue date to maturity date

DSM   =   Number of days from settlement date to maturity date

P   =   Dollar price per $100 par value

R   =   Annual interest rate (as a decimal)

Y   =   Annual Yield (as a decimal) on an investment with security held to maturity *

NOTE:   The first term calculates yield on invested dollars.  The second term converts this yield to a per annum basis.

---

*Annual Yield is also referred to as "Basis," "Yield Basis,"  or "Yield to Maturity."

# EXAMPLE

# FORMULA 3

## TAX EXEMPT NOTE

The following example illustrates the calculation of the yield on a tax exempt municipal note based on a dollar price.

| | | |
|---|---|---|
| Settlement Date | 03/07/95 | |
| Maturity Date | 11/03/95 | |
| Issue Date | 11/08/94 | |
| Day Count Basis | 30/360 | |
| A = 119 | (11/08/94 - 03/07/95) | |
| B = 360* | | |
| DIM = 355 | (11/08/94 - 11/03/95) | |
| DSM = 236* | (03/07/95 - 11/03/95) | |
| P = 100.068 | ($100.068) | |
| R = 0.06247 | (6.247%) | |
| Y = 0.06014973 | | |
| Yield = 6.015% | | |

---

*Municipal note dollar price calculations follow MSRB Rule G33. According to Rule G33; B is always 360 and DSM is calculated as DIM - A, not directly from the dates (this ensures that DIM will always equal A + DSM).

# FORMULA 4

[Price (given yield)]

$$P = \left[ \frac{100 + \left( \dfrac{DIM}{B} * R * 100 \right)}{1 + \left( \dfrac{DSM}{B} * Y \right)} \right] - \left[ \frac{A}{B} * R * 100 \right]$$

A   =   Number of days from issue date to settlement date (accrued days)

B   =   Number of days in a year (annual basis)

DIM   =   Number of days from issue date to maturity date

DSM   =   Number of days from settlement date to maturity date

P   =   Dollar price per $100 par value

R   =   Annual interest rate (as a decimal)

Y   =   Annual Yield (as a decimal) on an investment with security held to maturity *

NOTE:   The first term calculates present value of the maturity amount, including interest based upon the yield for the invested period.  The second term calculates accrued interest agreed to be paid to the seller.

---

*Annual Yield is also referred to as "Basis," "Yield Basis,"  or "Yield to Maturity."

# EXAMPLE

# FORMULA 4

## MUNICIPAL TAX EXEMPT NOTE

The following example illustrates the calculation of the dollar price on a municipal tax exempt note based on a particular yield.

| | | |
|---|---|---|
| Settlement Date | 02/07/92 | |
| Maturity Date | 04/13/92 | |
| Issue Date | 10/11/91 | |
| Day Count Basis | 30/360 | |
| A = 116 | (10/11/91 - 02/07/92) | |
| B = 360* | | |
| DIM = 182 | (10/11/91 - 04/13/92) | |
| DSM = 66* | (02/07/92 - 04/13/92) | |
| R = 0.0608 | (6.08%) | |
| Y = 0.0608 | (6.08%) | |
| P = 99.978403 | | |
| Dollar Price = 99.978 | | |

---

*Municipal note dollar price calculations follow MSRB Rule G33. According to Rule G33; B is always 360 and DSM is calculated as DIM - A, not directly from the dates (this ensures that DIM will always equal A + DSM).

$$\sum_{K=1}^{N} \frac{100 * \frac{R}{M}}{\left(1 + \frac{Y}{M}\right)^{K-1+\frac{DSC}{E}}}$$

## CALCULATIONS FOR SECURITIES WITH "REGULAR" PERIODIC INTEREST PAYMENTS

Securities considered "periodic" are those that are interest accruing or coupon bearing with interest payable at various time intervals (monthly, quarterly, semi-annually, annually, etc.) rather than solely at maturity.

The principle underlying periodic securities pricing is that the purchaser of a security is buying future payments of money, and is investing today only the present value of all those future payments, based upon a specified rate of return for his invested dollars (this total investment amount on present value includes accrued interest).

The basic formula for calculating the present value is:

$$PV = \frac{FV}{(1 + i)^n}$$

where:

FV = Amount to be received in the future (whether coupon or redemption value)

i = Interest rate per compounding period (i = 6% / 2 periods per year; i = 0.06 / 2 = 0.03)

n = Number of compounding periods

PV = Present value of the amount to be received in the future (total cost)

EXAMPLE:

The amount that must be invested to purchase a $100 security maturing in three years, paying interest semi-annually with an annual interest rate of 8% and purchased to yield 6%, would be determined as shown below using the standard present value formula.

Since the security has three years to maturity, there are six coupon payments (3 years @ 2 per year) and one par value payment. Each coupon payment is $4.00 and the par value payment is $100. The total cost of the security is the sum of the present values of each coupon and the present value of the par value.

Total cost equals:

|  | Present Value of Coupon 1 | $= \dfrac{4.00}{(1 + 0.03)^1}$ | = $ 3.8834951 |
| + | Present Value of Coupon 2 (paid after 2 compounding periods) | $= \dfrac{4.00}{(1 + 0.03)^2}$ | = $ 3.7703836 |
| + | Present Value of Coupon 3 (paid after 3 compounding periods) | $= \dfrac{4.00}{(1 + 0.03)^3}$ | = $ 3.6605666 |
| + | Present Value of Coupon 4 (paid after 4 compounding periods) | $= \dfrac{4.00}{(1 + 0.03)^4}$ | = $ 3.5539482 |
| + | Present Value of Coupon 5 (paid after 5 compounding periods) | $= \dfrac{4.00}{(1 + 0.03)^5}$ | = $ 3.4504351 |
| + | Present Value of Coupon 6 (paid after 6 compounding periods) | $= \dfrac{4.00}{(1 + 0.03)^6}$ | = $ 3.3499370 |

Total Present Value of All Coupon Payments $\qquad$ $ 21.6687655

| + | Present Value of Maturity Amount | $= \dfrac{100}{(1 + 0.03)^6}$ | = $ 83.7484256 |

Total Present Value (Dollar Price) $\qquad$ $ 105.4171911

It is important to recognize that the securities industry makes a distinction between price and yield calculations for securities with periodic interest payments with one coupon period or less to redemption (i.e., maturity, or call if pricing to call) and those with more than one coupon period to redemption. The reason for this distinction is that, traditionally with only one coupon period or less to redemption, computations are done based on simple interest rather than present value theory. Therefore, formulas 5 and 6 should be used for price and yield calculation when there is one coupon period or less to redemption.

Formulas 6 and 7 will calculate the dollar price for coupon securities with "regular" periodic interest payments. Formula 5 will calculate the yield to redemption based on a given dollar price for securities with less than one period to redemption. There is no formula to calculate yield directly for a security with more than one period to redemption. For a detailed explanation of why there is no formula and what should be done to calculate yield see the section entitled "Iteration Theory and Solving for Yield."

Formulas 5 and 6 are very similar to formulas 3 and 4. The basic difference between these two sets of formulas (3, 4 and 5, 6) is that in formulas 3 and 4 (interest at maturity, page 49) the security holder will be receiving interest in proportion to the length of time the security will be held as it relates to the annual interest rate. In the case of formulas 5 and 6, the bond holder will be receiving interest in proportion to the length of time the security is held as it relates to the coupon payment.

It should be noted that these formulas do not take into account securities with odd coupon periods. For price and yield calculations for securities with odd first and last coupon periods refer to the sections on "Odd Coupons."

The periodic formulas presented are:

| Formula Number | Description |
| --- | --- |
| 5 | Yield (given price) with one coupon period or less to redemption. |
| 6 | Price (given yield) with one coupon period or less to redemption. |
| 7 | Price (given yield) with more than one coupon period to redemption. |

# FORMULA 5

[Yield (given price) with one coupon period or less to redemption]

$$Y = \left[\frac{\left(\frac{RV}{100} + \frac{R}{M}\right) - \left(\frac{P}{100} + \left(\frac{A}{E} * \frac{R}{M}\right)\right)}{\frac{P}{100} + \left(\frac{A}{E} * \frac{R}{M}\right)}\right] * \left[\frac{M * E}{DSR}\right]$$

A = Number of days from beginning of coupon period to settlement date (accrued days)

DSR = Number of days from settlement date to redemption date (maturity date, call date, put date, etc.)

E = Number of days in coupon period

M = Number of coupon periods per year (standard for the particular security involved)

P = Dollar price per $100 par value

R = Annual interest rate (as a decimal)

RV = Redemption value of the security per $100 par value (RV = 100, except in those cases where call or put features must be considered)

Y = Annual Yield (as a decimal) on investment with security held to redemption*

NOTE: The first term calculates yield on invested dollars. The second term converts this yield to a per annum basis.

---

*Annual Yield is also referred to as "Basis," "Yield Basis," or "Yield to Maturity."

# EXAMPLE

# FORMULA 5

## U.S. TREASURY NOTE

The following example illustrates the calculation of the yield on a U.S. Treasury Note given a dollar price and the settlement date is less than one period away from the maturity date.

| | | |
|---|---|---|
| Settlement Date | 02/07/92 | |
| Maturity Date | 05/15/92 | |
| Day Count Basis | Actual/Actual | |
| A = 84 | (11/15/91 to 02/07/92) | |
| DSR = 98 | (02/07/92 to 05/15/92) | |
| E = 182 | (11/15/91 to 05/15/92) | |
| M = 2 | (semi-annual) | |
| P = 99.875 | $(99^{28}\!/_{32})$ | |
| R = 0.0475 | $(4\frac{3}{4}\%)$ | |
| RV = 100 | | |
| Y = 0.05164134 | | |
| Yield = 5.164% | | |

# FORMULA 6

[Price (given yield) with one coupon period or less to redemption]

$$P = \left[ \frac{RV + \dfrac{100*R}{M}}{1 + \left( \dfrac{DSR}{E} * \dfrac{Y}{M} \right)} \right] - \left[ \frac{A}{E} * \frac{100*R}{M} \right]$$

A = Number of days from beginning of coupon period to settlement date (accrued days)

DSR = Number of days from settlement date to redemption date (maturity date, call date, put date, etc.)

E = Number of days in coupon period

M = Number of coupon periods per year (standard for the particular security involved)

P = Dollar price per $100 par value

R = Annual interest rate (as a decimal)

RV = Redemption value of the security per $100 par value (RV = 100, except in those cases where call or put features must be considered)

Y = Annual Yield (as a decimal) on investment with security held to redemption*

NOTE: The first term calculates present value of the redemption amount, including interest, based upon the yield for the invested period. The second term calculates the accrued interest agreed to be paid to the seller.

---

*Annual Yield is also referred to as "Basis," "Yield Basis," or "Yield to Maturity."

# EXAMPLE                                    # FORMULA 6

## MUNICIPAL BOND

The following example illustrates the calculation of the dollar price given a yield for a municipal bond with its settlement date within one period of the maturity.

| | | |
|---|---|---|
| Settlement Date | 02/07/93 | |
| Maturity Date | 08/01/93 | |
| Day Count Basis | 30/360 | |
| A = 6 | (02/01/93 - 02/07/93) | |
| DSR = 174* | (02/07/93 - 08/01/93) | |
| E = 180* | (02/01/93 - 08/01/93) | |
| M = 2 | (semi-annual) | |
| R = 0.045 | (4½%) | |
| RV = 100 | | |
| Y = 0.0535 | (5.35%) | |
| P = 99.597632 | | |
| Dollar Price = 99.597 | | |

---

*Municipal bond dollar price calculations follow MSRB Rule G33. According to Rule G33; E is always 180 (there are 360 days in a year and 2 coupon payments per year) and DSR is calculated as E - A, not directly from the dates (this ensures that E will always equal A + DSR).

# FORMULA 7

[Price (given yield) with more than one coupon period to redemption]

$$P = \left[ \frac{RV}{\left(1 + \frac{Y}{M}\right)^{N-1+\frac{DSC}{E}}} \right] + \left[ \sum_{K=1}^{N} \frac{100 * \frac{R}{M}}{\left(1 + \frac{Y}{M}\right)^{K-1+\frac{DSC}{E}}} \right] - \left[ 100 * \frac{R}{M} * \frac{A}{E} \right]$$

A = Number of days from beginning of coupon period to settlement date (accrued days)

DSC = Number of days from settlement date to next coupon date

E = Number of days in coupon period in which the settlement date falls

K = A summation counter

M = Number of coupon periods per year (standard for the particular security involved)

N = Number of coupons payable between settlement date and redemption date (maturity date, call date, put date, etc.) (If this number contains a fractional part, raise it to the next whole number - i.e. 2½ = 3)

P = Dollar price per $100 par value

R = Annual interest rate (as a decimal)

RV = Redemption value of the security per $100 par value (RV = 100, except in those cases where call or put features must be considered)

Y = Annual Yield (as a decimal) on investment with security held to redemption*

NOTE: The first term calculates present value of the redemption amount, not including interest. The second term calculates present values for all future coupon payments. The third term calculates the accrued interest agreed to be paid to the seller.

---

*Annual Yield is also referred to as "Basis," "Yield Basis," or "Yield to Maturity."

# EXAMPLE                                             FORMULA 7

## CORPORATE BOND

The following example illustrates the calculation of a dollar price for a corporate bond given a yield to maturity, with the settlement date more than one coupon period from the maturity.

| | | |
|---|---|---|
| Settlement Date | 02/25/93 | |
| Maturity Date | 12/15/04 | |
| Day Count Basis | 30/360 | |
| A = 70 | (12/15/92 - 02/25/93) | |
| DSC = 110 | (02/25/93 - 06/15/93) | |
| E = 180 | (12/15/92 - 06/15/93) | |
| M = 2 | (semi-annual) | |
| N = 24 | | |
| R = 0.05875 | (5⅞%) | |
| RV = 100 | | |
| Y = 0.0646 | (6.46%) | |
| P = 95.208327 | | |
| Dollar Price = 95.208 | | |

$$\frac{100 * R * \dfrac{DFC}{E}}{\left(1 + \dfrac{Y}{M}\right)}$$

## ODD FIRST COUPONS

The length of the first coupon period for coupon bearing securities is sometimes other than the "normal" length for that security. The odd coupon can be either short (less than a normal length coupon) or long (greater than a normal length coupon). Both long and short coupons should be taken into account when calculating the price or yield and accrued interest if the settlement date occurs within the odd period. If the settlement date occurs after the odd first period, then the formulas for "regular" periodic payments should be used. For price and yield computation on treasury and agency securities, the odd period is considered. For price and yield computations in municipal securities refer to Appendix A - MSRB Rule G-33. Calculations of price and yield for corporate bonds with odd coupons have traditionally followed the accepted practice for municipal bonds. We now recommend that the odd coupon be taken into consideration in the corporate area.

Presented on the following pages as Formulas 8 and 9 are modifications to Formula 7, which take into account odd first coupon periods. For municipal securities, as required in Rule G-33, Formula 7 (unmodified) should be used, ignoring the odd coupon, for price calculation; but, the odd coupon should be considered for the purpose of adding accrued interest to the calculated principal to arrive at the total cost of the security. A full explanation of the interest accrual method for odd coupons can be found in the "Interest-Discount Calculations" section of this book.

| Formula Number | Description |
|---|---|
| 8* | Price (given yield) with an odd short first coupon |
| 9* | Price (given yield) with an odd long first coupon |

---

*For "Yield (given price)" calculations, a method of iteration must be used (see the section "Iteration Theory and Solving for Yield").

# FORMULA 8

[Odd short first coupon - Price (given yield)] [Settlement Date in odd period]

$$P = \left[ \frac{RV}{\left(1 + \frac{Y}{M}\right)^{N-1+\frac{DSC}{E}}} \right] + \left[ \frac{100 * \frac{R}{M} * \frac{DFC}{E}}{\left(1 + \frac{Y}{M}\right)^{\frac{DSC}{E}}} \right] + \left[ \sum_{K=2}^{N} \frac{100 * \frac{R}{M}}{\left(1 + \frac{Y}{M}\right)^{K-1+\frac{DSC}{E}}} \right] - \left[ 100 * \frac{R}{M} * \frac{A}{E} \right]$$

A = Number of days from beginning of coupon period to settlement date (accrued days)

DFC = Number of days from the beginning of the odd first coupon period (dated date) to the first coupon date

DSC = Number of days from settlement date to first coupon date

E = Number of days in quasi-coupon period in which the settlement date falls

K = A summation counter

M = Number of coupon periods per year (standard for the particular security involved)

N = Number of coupons payable between settlement date and redemption date (maturity date, call date, put date, etc.) (If this number contains a fractional part, raise it to the next whole number - i.e. 2½=3)

P = Dollar price per $100 par value

R = Annual interest rate (as a decimal)

RV = Redemption value of the security per $100 par value (RV = 100, except in those cases where call or put features must be considered)

Y = Annual Yield (as a decimal) on investment with security held to redemption

NOTE: The first term calculates present value of the redemption amount, not including interest. The second term calculates the present value of the odd short first coupon. The third term calculates present values for all other future coupon payments. The fourth term calculates the accrued interest agreed to be paid to the seller.

NOTE: For a full explanation of quasi-coupon periods and accrued interest for an odd coupon period refer to the "Interest-Discount Calculations" section of this book.

---

NOTE: This formula does not apply to municipal securities.

# EXAMPLE                                   FORMULA 8

## TREASURY BOND

The following example illustrates the calculation of a dollar price given a yield for a Treasury Bond with an odd short first coupon.

| | | |
|---|---|---|
| Settlement Date | | 11/11/92 |
| Maturity Date | | 03/01/05 |
| Issue/Dated Date | | 10/15/92 |
| First Coupon Date | | 03/01/93 |
| Day Count Basis | | Actual/Actual |
| A | = 27 | (10/15/92 - 11/11/92) |
| DFC | = 137 | (10/15/92 - 03/01/93) |
| DSC | = 110 | (11/11/92 - 03/01/93) |
| E | = 181* | (09/01/92 - 03/01/93) |
| M | = 2 | (semi-annual) |
| N | = 25 | (11/11/92 - 03/01/05) |
| R | = 0.0785 | (7.85%) |
| RV | = 100.000 | |
| Y | = 0.0625 | (6¼%) |
| P | = 113.597717 | |
| Dollar Price | = 113.597717 | |

---

*This figure is based on the quasi-coupon date of 9/1/92.

# FORMULA 9

[Odd long first coupon - Price (given yield)] [Settlement Date in odd period]

$$P = \left[ \frac{RV}{\left(1 + \frac{Y}{M}\right)^{N + Nqf + \frac{DSC}{E}}} \right] + \left[ \frac{100 * \frac{R}{M} * \left[ \sum_{i=1}^{NCF} \frac{DFC_i}{NLF_i} \right]}{\left(1 + \frac{Y}{M}\right)^{Nqf + \frac{DSC}{E}}} \right] + \left[ \sum_{K=1}^{N} \frac{100 * \frac{R}{M}}{\left(1 + \frac{Y}{M}\right)^{K + Nqf + \frac{DSC}{E}}} \right] - \left[ 100 * \frac{R}{M} * \left[ \sum_{i=1}^{NCF} \frac{A_i}{NLF_i} \right] \right]$$

$A_i$ = Number of accrued days for the ith quasi-coupon period within the odd period (accrued days)

$DFC_i$ = Number of days from dated date to first quasi-coupon (i=1) or number of days in quasi coupon (i=2,3,...,NC)

DSC = Number of days from settlement date to next quasi-coupon date or next coupon date

E = Number of days in quasi-coupon period, or regular coupon period, in which the settlement date falls

i = A summation counter for interest computation

K = A summation counter

M = Number of coupon periods per year

N = Number of coupons periods between <u>the first real coupon date</u> and redemption date (maturity date, call date, put date, etc.)

NCF = Number of quasi-coupon periods that fit in odd period. (If this number contains a fractional part, raise it to the next whole number.)

$NLF_i$ = Normal length in days of the full ith quasi-coupon period within odd period

Nqf = Number of <u>whole</u> quasi-coupon periods between settlement date and first coupon (this may be zero)

P = Dollar price per $100 par value

R = Annual interest rate (as a decimal)

RV = Redemption value of the security per $100 par value (RV = 100, except in those cases where call or put features must be considered)

Y = Annual Yield (as a decimal) on investment with security held to redemption

NOTE: The first term calculates the present value of the redemption amount, not including interest. The second term calculates the present value of the odd long first coupon. The third term calculates present values for all other future coupon payments. The fourth term calculates the accrued interest agreed to be paid to the seller.

NOTE: For a full explanation of quasi-coupon periods and accrued interest for an odd coupon period refer to the "Interest-Discount Calculations" section of this book.

This formula does not apply to municipal securities.

# EXAMPLE

# FORMULA 9

## TREASURY BOND

The following example illustrates the calculation of a dollar price given a yield for a Treasury Bond with an odd long first coupon.

| | | |
|---|---|---|
| Settlement Date | | 11/11/92 |
| Maturity Date | | 03/01/05 |
| Issue/Dated Date | | 06/15/92 |
| First Coupon Date | | 03/01/93 |
| Day Count Basis | | Actual/Actual |
| $A_1$ | = 78* | (06/15/92 - 09/01/92) |
| $A_2$ | = 71* | (09/01/92 - 11/11/92) |
| $DFC_1$ | = 78* | (06/15/92 - 09/01/92) |
| $DFC_2$ | = 181* | (09/01/92 - 03/01/93) |
| $DSC$ | = 110 | (11/11/92 - 03/01/93) |
| $E$ | = 181* | (09/01/92 - 03/01/93) |
| $M$ | = 2 | (semi-annual) |
| $N$ | = 24 | (03/01/93 - 03/01/05) |
| $NCF$ | = 2 | (06/15/92 - 03/01/93) |
| $NLF_1$ | = 184* | (03/01/92 - 09/01/92) |
| $NLF_2$ | = 181* | (09/01/92 - 03/01/93) |
| $Nqf$ | = 0 | (11/11/92 - 03/01/93) |
| $R$ | = 0.0935 | (9.35%) |
| $RV$ | = 100.000 | |
| $Y$ | = 0.0775 | (7¾%) |
| $P$ | = 112.478106 | |
| Dollar Price | = 112.478106 | |

---

*These figures are based on the quasi-coupon dates of 3/1/92 and 9/1/92.

$$\frac{100 * R * \dfrac{DLC}{NL}}{\left(1 + \dfrac{Y}{M}\right)}$$

## ODD LAST COUPONS

The length of the last coupon period for coupon bearing securities is sometimes other than the "normal" length for that security. The odd coupon can be either short (less than a normal length coupon) or long (greater than a normal length coupon). Both short and long coupons should be considered when calculating the price or yield and accrued interest. For price and yield computation on treasury and agency securities, the odd period, if it exists, is taken into account. For price and yield computations in municipal securities refer to Appendix A - MSRB Rule G-33. Calculations of price and yield for corporate bonds with odd coupons have traditionally followed the accepted practice for municipal bonds. We now recommend that the odd last coupon be taken into account in the corporate area.

Formulas 10, 11, 12, and 13 should be used when the settlement date falls in the last coupon period (the settlement date is on or after the last coupon date before redemption). Formulas 14 and 15 should be used when the settlement date falls before the last coupon date before redemption.

A full explanation of the interest accrual method for odd last coupons can be found in the "Interest-Discount Calculations" section of this book.

| Formula Number | Description |
|---|---|
| 10 | Yield (given price) with an odd short last coupon and the settlement date in the odd period |
| 11 | Price (given yield) with an odd short last coupon and the settlement date in the odd period |
| 12 | Yield (given price) with an odd long last coupon and the settlement date in the odd period |
| 13 | Price (given yield) with an odd long last coupon and the settlement date in the odd period |
| 14* | Price (given yield) with an odd short last coupon and more than one period to redemption |
| 15* | Price (given yield) with an odd long last coupon and more than one period to redemption |

---

*For "Yield (given price)" calculations, a method of iteration must be used (see the section "Iteration Theory and Solving for Yield").

# FORMULA 10

[Odd short last coupon - Yield (given price) with one coupon period or less to redemption]

$$Y = \left[ \frac{\left( \frac{RV}{100} + \left( \frac{R}{M} * \frac{DLC}{E} \right) \right) - \left( \frac{P}{100} + \left( \frac{A}{E} * \frac{R}{M} \right) \right)}{\frac{P}{100} + \left( \frac{A}{E} * \frac{R}{M} \right)} \right] * \left[ \frac{M * E}{DSR} \right]$$

A = Number of days from last coupon date before redemption to settlement date (accrued days)

DLC = Number of days from last coupon date before redemption to redemption

DSR = Number of days from settlement date to redemption date (maturity date, call date, put date, etc.)

E = Number of days in the quasi-coupon period

M = Number of coupon periods per year (standard for the particular security involved)

P = Dollar price per $100 par value

R = Annual interest rate (as a decimal)

RV = Redemption value of the security per $100 par value (RV = 100, except in those cases where call or put features must be considered)

Y = Annual Yield (as a decimal) on investment with security held to redemption

NOTE: The first term calculates yield on invested dollars. The second term converts this yield to a per annum basis.

NOTE: In this case of odd short last coupon with less than one coupon to redemption, day counting for quasi-coupon determination and interest computation starts from last coupon date prior to settlement and proceeds forward, rather than backward, from maturity date. Also see section on "Interest-Discount Calculation."

# EXAMPLE

# FORMULA 10

## MEDIUM TERM NOTE

The following example illustrates the calculation of the yield on a corporate medium term note given a dollar price. The settlement date is less than one coupon period away from maturity date.

| | |
|---|---|
| Settlement Date | 02/20/92 |
| Maturity Date | 05/15/92 |
| Last Coupon Date Before Redemption | 02/15/92 |
| Day Count Basis | 30/360 |

| | | |
|---|---|---|
| A | = 5 | (02/15/92 - 02/20/92) |
| DLC | = 90 | (02/15/92 - 05/15/92) |
| DSR | = 85 | (02/20/92 - 05/15/92) |
| E | = 180 | (11/15/91 - 08/15/92) |
| M | = 2 | (semi-annual) |
| P | = 100.5 | (100½) |
| R | = 0.07125 | (7⅛%) |
| RV | = 100 | |
| Y | = 0.0497754 | |
| Yield | = 4.978% | |

# FORMULA 11

[Odd short last coupon - Price (given yield) with one coupon period or less to redemption]

$$P = \left[ \frac{RV + \left( \frac{100 * R}{M} * \frac{DLC}{E} \right)}{1 + \left( \frac{DSR}{E} * \frac{Y}{M} \right)} \right] - \left[ \frac{A}{E} * \frac{100 * R}{M} \right]$$

A = Number of days from last coupon date before redemption to settlement date (accrued days)

DLC = Number of days from last coupon date before redemption to redemption

DSR = Number of days from settlement date to redemption date (maturity date, call date, put date, etc.)

E = Number of days in the quasi-coupon period

M = Number of coupon periods per year

P = Dollar price per $100 par value

R = Annual interest rate (as a decimal)

RV = Redemption value of the security per $100 par value (RV = 100, except in those cases where call or put features must be considered)

Y = Annual Yield (as a decimal) on investment with security held to redemption*

NOTE: The first term calculates present value of the redemption amount, including interest, based upon the yield for the invested period. The second term calculates the accrued interest agreed to be paid to the seller.

NOTE: In this case of odd short last coupon with less than one coupon to redemption, day counting for quasi-coupon determination and interest computation starts from last coupon date prior to settlement and proceeds forward, rather than backward, from maturity date. Also see section on "Interest-Discount Calculation."

---

*Annual Yield is also referred to as "Basis," "Yield Basis," or "Yield to Maturity."

# EXAMPLE                                    FORMULA 11

## MEDIUM TERM NOTE

The following example illustrates the calculation of the price on a corporate medium term note given a yield. The settlement date is less than one coupon period away from the maturity date.

| | | |
|---|---|---|
| Settlement Date | 02/07/93 | |
| Maturity Date | 08/01/93 | |
| Last Coupon Date Before Redemption | 02/04/93 | |
| Day Count Basis | 30/360 | |
| A = 3 | (02/04/93 - 02/07/93) | |
| DLC = 177 | (02/04/93 - 08/01/93) | |
| DSR = 174 | (02/07/93 - 08/01/93) | |
| E = 180 | (02/04/93 - 08/04/93) | |
| M = 2 | (semi-annual) | |
| R = 0.065 | (6½%) | |
| RV = 100 | | |
| Y = 0.0535 | (5.35%) | |
| P = 100.540457 | | |
| Dollar Price = 100.540 | | |

# FORMULA 12

[Odd long last coupon - Yield (given price) with settlement one coupon or less to redemption]

$$Y = \left[ \frac{\left( RV + \left( \left( \sum_{i=1}^{NCL} \frac{DLC_i}{NLL_i} \right) * \frac{100 * R}{M} \right) \right) - \left( P + \left( \left( \sum_{i=1}^{NCL} \frac{A_i}{NLL_i} \right) * \frac{100 * R}{M} \right) \right)}{P + \left( \left( \sum_{i=1}^{NCL} \frac{A_i}{NLL_i} \right) * \frac{100 * R}{M} \right)} \right] * \left[ \frac{M}{\sum_{i=1}^{NCL} \frac{DSC_i}{NLL_i}} \right]$$

$A_i$ = Number of accrued days for the $i$th quasi-coupon period within the odd period

$DLC_i$ = Number of days counted in the $i$th quasi-coupon period as delimited by the total length of the actual coupon period

$DSC_i$ = Number of days from settlement date (or beginning of quasi-coupon period) to next quasi-coupon within odd period (or to redemption date) for the $i$th quasi-coupon period

$i$ = A summation counter

$M$ = Number of coupon periods per year (standard for the particular security involved)

$NCL$ = Number of quasi-coupon periods that fit in odd period. (If this number contains a fractional part, raise it to the next whole number - i.e. $2\frac{1}{2} = 3$).

$NLL_i$ = Normal Length in days of the full $i$th quasi-coupon period within odd last period

$P$ = Dollar price per $100 par value

$R$ = Annual interest rate (as a decimal)

$RV$ = Redemption value (call price, put price, or maturity value expressed per $100 par value)

$Y$ = Annual Yield on investment with security held to redemption (as a decimal)*

NOTE: The first term represents the yield on investment for the period of investment. The second term converts this yield to a per annum basis.

NOTE: In this case of odd long last coupon with less than one coupon to redemption, day counting for quasi-coupon determination and interest computation starts from last coupon date prior to settlement and proceeds forward, rather than backward, from maturity date. Also see section on "Interest-Discount Calculation."

---

*Annual Yield is also referred to as "Basis," "Yield Basis," or "Yield to Maturity."

# EXAMPLE                                          FORMULA 12

**BOND**

The following example illustrates the calculation of a yield given a dollar price for a bond with an odd last coupon and one coupon or less to redemption.

| | | |
|---|---|---|
| Settlement Date | 04/20/93 | |
| Maturity Date | 06/15/93 | |
| Last Coupon Date Before Redemption | 10/15/92 | |
| Day Count Basis | 30/360 | |
| $A_1$ = 180 | (10/15/92 - 04/15/93) | |
| $A_2$ = 5 | (04/15/93 - 04/20/93) | |
| $DLC_1$ = 180 | (10/15/92 - 04/15/93) | |
| $DLC_2$ = 60 | (04/15/93 - 06/15/93) | |
| $DSC_1$ = 0 | (N/A) | |
| $DSC_2$ = 55 | (04/20/93 - 06/15/93) | |
| M = 2 | (semi-annual) | |
| NCL = 2 | (10/15/92 - 06/15/93) | |
| $NLL_1$ = 180 | (10/15/92 - 04/15/93) | |
| $NLL_2$ = 180 | (04/15/93 - 10/15/93) | |
| P = 99.875 | ($99.875) | |
| R = 0.0375 | (3¾%) | |
| RV = 100 | | |
| Y = 0.04487317 | | |
| Yield = 4.487% | | |

# FORMULA 13

[Odd long last coupon - Price (given yield) with settlement one coupon or less to redemption]

$$P = \left[ \frac{RV + \left( \left( \sum_{i=1}^{NCL} \frac{DLC_i}{NLL_i} \right) * \frac{100 * R}{M} \right)}{1 + \left( \left( \sum_{i=1}^{NCL} \frac{DSC_i}{NLL_i} \right) * \frac{Y}{M} \right)} \right] - \left[ \left( \sum_{i=1}^{NCL} \frac{A_i}{NLL_i} \right) * \frac{100 * R}{M} \right]$$

$A_i$ = Number of accrued days for the ith quasi-coupon period within odd period counting forward from last interest date before redemption

$DLC_i$ = Number of days counted in the ith quasi-coupon period as delimited by the length of the actual coupon period

$DSC_i$ = Number of days from settlement date (or beginning of quasi-coupon period) to next quasi-coupon within odd period (or to redemption date) for the ith quasi-coupon period

$i$ = A summation counter

$M$ = Number of coupon periods per year (standard for the particular security involved)

$NCL$ = Number of quasi-coupon periods that fit in odd period (If this number contains a fractional part, raise it to the next whole number - i.e. $2\frac{1}{2} = 3$)

$NLL_i$ = Normal length in days of the ith quasi-coupon period within odd last coupon period

$P$ = Dollar price per $100 par value

$R$ = Annual interest rate (as a decimal)

$RV$ = Redemption value (call price, put price, or maturity value expressed per $100 par value)

$Y$ = Annual Yield on investment with security held to redemption (as a decimal)*

NOTE: The first term represents the present value of the redemption amount. The second term represents the accrued interest agreed to be paid to the seller.

NOTE: In this case of odd long last coupon with one coupon or less to redemption, day counting for quasi-coupon determination and interest computation starts from last coupon date prior to settlement and proceeds forward, rather than backward, from maturity date. Also see section on "Interest-Discount Calculation."

---

*Annual Yield is also referred to as "Basis," "Yield Basis," or "Yield to Maturity."

## BOND

The following example illustrates the calculation of a dollar price given the yield for a bond with an odd long last coupon and one coupon or less to redemption.

| | | |
|---|---|---|
| Settlement Date | 02/07/93 | |
| Maturity Date | 06/15/93 | |
| Last Interest Date Before Redemption | 10/15/92 | |
| Day Count Basis | 30/360 | |
| $A_1$ = 112 | (10/15/92 - 02/07/93) | |
| $A_2$ = 0 | | |
| $DLC_1$ = 180 | (10/15/92 - 04/15/93) | |
| $DLC_2$ = 60 | (04/15/93 - 06/15/93) | |
| $DSC_1$ = 68 | (02/07/93 - 04/15/93) | |
| $DSC_2$ = 60 | (04/15/93 - 06/15/93) | |
| M = 2 | (semi-annual) | |
| NCL = 2 | (10/15/92 - 06/15/93) | |
| $NLL_1$ = 180 | (10/15/92 - 04/15/93) | |
| $NLL_2$ = 180 | (04/15/93 - 10/15/93) | |
| R = 0.0375 | (3¾%) | |
| RV = 100 | | |
| Y = 0.0405 | (4.05%) | |
| P = 99.878286 | | |
| Dollar Price = 99.878 | | |

# FORMULA 14

[Odd short last coupon - Price (given yield) with more than one coupon period to redemption]

$$P = \left[ \frac{RV}{\left(1 + \frac{Y}{M}\right)^{N-1+\frac{DSC}{E}+\frac{DLC}{NLL}}} \right] + \left[ \sum_{K=1}^{N} \frac{100 * \frac{R}{M}}{\left(1 + \frac{Y}{M}\right)^{K-1+\frac{DSC}{E}}} \right] + \left[ \frac{100 * \frac{R}{M} * \frac{DLC}{NLL}}{\left(1 + \frac{Y}{M}\right)^{N-1+\frac{DSC}{E}+\frac{DLC}{NLL}}} \right] - \left[ 100 * \frac{R}{M} * \frac{A}{E} \right]$$

A = Number of days from beginning of coupon period to settlement date (accrued days)

DLC = Number of days from last coupon date before redemption to redemption date

DSC = Number of days from settlement date to next coupon date

E = Number of days in coupon period in which the settlement date falls

K = A summation counter

M = Number of coupon periods per year (standard for the particular security involved)

N = Number of coupons payable between settlement date and last coupon date before redemption (maturity date, call date, put date, etc.) (If this number contains a fractional part, raise it to the next whole number - i.e. 2½ = 3)

NLL = Normal length in days of the full quasi-coupon period in which the odd last period falls

P = Dollar price per $100 par value

R = Annual interest rate (as a decimal)

RV = Redemption value of the security per $100 par value (RV = 100, except in those cases where call or put features must be considered)

Y = Annual Yield (as a decimal) on investment with security held to redemption*

NOTE: The first term calculates present value of the redemption amount, not including interest. The second term calculates present values for all future coupon payments except the last coupon payment. The third term calculates the present value of the last coupon payment. The fourth term calculates the accrued interest agreed to be paid to the seller.

---

*Annual Yield is also referred to as "Basis," "Yield Basis," or "Yield to Maturity."

## CORPORATE BOND

The following example illustrates the calculation of a dollar price for a corporate bond given a yield to maturity, with the settlement date further than one coupon period from maturity.

| | | |
|---|---|---|
| Settlement Date | | 02/25/93 |
| Maturity Date | | 06/01/05 |
| Last Interest Date Before Redemption | | 12/15/04 |
| Day Count Basis | | 30/360 |
| A | = 70 | (12/15/92 - 02/25/93) |
| DLC | = 166 | (12/15/04 - 06/01/05) |
| DSC | = 110 | (02/25/93 - 06/15/93) |
| E | = 180 | (12/15/92 - 06/15/93) |
| M | = 2 | (semi-annual) |
| N | = 24 | (02/25/93 - 12/15/04) |
| NLL | = 180 | (12/15/04 - 06/15/05) |
| R | = 0.06875 | (6⅞%) |
| RV | = 100 | |
| Y | = 0.0725 | (7¼%) |
| P | = 96.974120 | |
| Dollar Price | = 96.974 | |

# FORMULA 15

[Odd long last coupon - Price (given yield) with more than one coupon period to redemption]

$$P = \left[ \frac{RV}{\left(1+\frac{Y}{M}\right)^{N-1+\frac{DSC}{E}+Nql+\frac{DLQ}{LQL}}} \right] + \left[ \sum_{K=1}^{N} \frac{100*\frac{R}{M}}{\left(1+\frac{Y}{M}\right)^{K-1+\frac{DSC}{E}}} \right] + \left[ \frac{100*\frac{R}{M}*\left(\sum_{i=1}^{NCL}\frac{DLC_i}{NLL_i}\right)}{\left(1+\frac{Y}{M}\right)^{N-1+\frac{DSC}{E}+Nql+\frac{DLQ}{LQL}}} \right] - \left[ 100*\frac{R}{M}*\frac{A}{E} \right]$$

A = Number of days from beginning of coupon period to settlement date (accrued days)

$DLC_i$ = Number of days counted in the ith quasi-coupon period as delimited by the length of the actual coupon period

DLQ = Number of days counted in the last (NCL[th]) quasi-coupon period within the odd last period (DLQ = $DLC_i$ where i = NCL).

DSC = Number of days from settlement date to next coupon date

E = Number of days in coupon period in which the settlement date falls

i = A summation counter

K = A summation counter

LQL = Normal length in days of the last (NCL[th]) quasi-coupon period within the odd last period (LQL = $NLL_i$ where i = NCL).

M = Number of coupon periods per year (standard for the particular security involved)

N = Number of coupons payable between settlement date and last coupon date before redemption (maturity date, call date, etc.) (If this number contains a fractional part, raise it to the next whole number - i.e. 2½ = 3)

NCL = Number of quasi-coupon periods that fit in odd last period. (If this number contains a fractional part, raise it to the next whole number.)

$NLL_i$ = Normal length in days of the full ith quasi-coupon period within odd last period

Nql = Number of whole quasi-coupon periods between last coupon date before redemption and the redemption date

P = Dollar price per $100 par value

R = Annual interest rate (as a decimal)

RV = Redemption value of the security per $100 par value (RV = 100, except in those cases where call or put features must be considered)

Y = Annual Yield (as a decimal) on investment with security held to redemption*

NOTE: The first term calculates present value of the redemption amount, not including interest. The second term calculates present values for all future coupon payments except the last coupon payment. The third term calculates the present value of the last coupon payment. The fourth term calculates the accrued interest agreed to be paid to the seller.

---

*Annual Yield is also referred to as "Basis," "Yield Basis," or "Yield to Maturity."

# EXAMPLE

## FORMULA 15

### MEDIUM TERM NOTE

The following example illustrates the calculation of a dollar price for a medium term note given a yield to maturity, with the settlement date further than one coupon period from maturity.

| | | |
|---|---|---|
| Settlement Date | | 02/25/93 |
| Maturity Date | | 09/15/04 |
| Last Interest Date Before Redemption | | 12/15/03 |
| Day Count Basis | | 30/360 |
| $A$ = | 70 | (12/15/92 - 02/25/93) |
| $DLC_1$ = | 180 | (12/15/03 - 06/15/04) |
| $DLC_2$ = | 90 | (06/15/04 - 09/15/04) |
| $DLQ$ = | 90 | (06/15/04 - 09/15/04) |
| $DSC$ = | 110 | (02/25/93 - 06/15/93) |
| $E$ = | 180 | (12/15/92 - 06/15/93) |
| $LQL$ = | 180 | (06/15/04 - 12/15/04) |
| $M$ = | 2 | (semi-annual) |
| $N$ = | 22 | (02/25/93 - 12/15/03) |
| $NCL$ = | 2 | (12/15/03 - 09/15/04) |
| $NLL_1$ = | 180 | (12/15/03 - 06/15/04) |
| $NLL_2$ = | 180 | (06/15/04 - 12/15/04) |
| $Nql$ = | 1 | (12/15/03 - 09/15/04) |
| $R$ = | 0.06875 | (6⅞%) |
| $RV$ = | 100 | |
| $Y$ = | 0.0893 | (8.93%) |
| $P$ = | 85.334452 | |
| Dollar Price = | 85.334 | |

$$100 * \dfrac{R}{M} * \dfrac{\left( \displaystyle\sum_{i=1}^{NCL} \dfrac{DCL_i}{NLL_i} \right)}{\left(1 + \dfrac{Y}{M}\right)^{N + \frac{DSC}{E} + Nql + \frac{DLC}{NLL}}}$$

## ODD FIRST AND LAST COUPONS

The length of the first and last coupon period for coupon bearing securities is sometimes other than the "normal" length for that security. The odd coupons can be either short (less than a normal length coupon) or long (greater than a normal length coupon). If the settlement date falls within the odd first coupon, then both the odd first and odd last coupons should be taken into account when calculating the price or yield and accrued interest. If the settlement date is after the odd first coupon period, then the formulas in the section "Odd Last Coupons" should be used. For price and yield computation on treasury and agency securities, the odd periods are considered. For price and yield computations in municipal securities refer to Appendix A - MSRB Rule G-33. Calculations of price and yield for corporate bonds with odd coupons have traditionally followed the accepted practice for municipal bonds. We now recommend that the odd coupon be taken into consideration in the corporate area.

| Formula Number | Description |
| --- | --- |
| 16* | Price (given yield) with an odd short first and odd short last coupon with the settlement date in the odd first period |
| 17* | Price (given yield) with an odd long first and odd short last coupon with the settlement date in the odd first period |
| 18* | Price (given yield) with an odd short first and odd long last coupon with the settlement date in the odd first period |
| 19* | Price (given yield) with an odd long first and odd long last coupon with the settlement date in the odd first period |

---

*For "Yield (given price)" calculations, a method of iteration must be used (see section "Iteration Theory and Solving for Yield").

# FORMULA 16

[Odd short first and odd short last coupons - Price (given yield)] [Settlement date in odd first period]

$$P = \left[\frac{RV}{\left(1+\frac{Y}{M}\right)^{N-1+\frac{DSC}{E}+\frac{DLC}{NLL}}}\right] + \left[\frac{100*\frac{R}{M}*\frac{DFC}{E}}{\left(1+\frac{Y}{M}\right)^{\frac{DSC}{E}}} + \sum_{K=2}^{N}\frac{100*\frac{R}{M}}{\left(1+\frac{Y}{M}\right)^{K-1+\frac{DSC}{E}}}\right] + \left[\frac{100*\frac{R}{M}*\frac{DLC}{NLL}}{\left(1+\frac{Y}{M}\right)^{N-1+\frac{DSC}{E}+\frac{DLC}{NLL}}}\right] - \left[100*\frac{R}{M}*\frac{A}{E}\right]$$

A = Number of days from beginning of coupon period to settlement date (accrued days)

DFC = Number of days from the beginning of the odd first coupon (dated date) to the first coupon date

DLC = Number of days from last coupon date before redemption to redemption date

DSC = Number of days from settlement date to first coupon date

E = Number of days in quasi-coupon period in which the settlement date falls

K = A summation counter

M = Number of coupon periods per year (standard for the particular security involved)

N = Number of coupons payable between settlement date and last coupon before redemption date. (If this number contains a fractional part, raise it to the next whole number - i.e. 2½ = 3)

NLL = Normal length in days of the full quasi-coupon period in which the odd last period falls

P = Dollar price per $100 par value

R = Annual interest rate (as a decimal)

RV = Redemption value of the security per $100 par value (RV = 100, except in those cases where call or put features must be considered)

Y = Annual Yield (as a decimal) on investment with security held to redemption

NOTE: The first term calculates present value of the redemption amount, not including interest. The second term calculates the present value of the first coupon payment. The third term calculates present values for all future coupon payments except the first and last coupon payments. The fourth term calculates the present value of the last coupon payment. The fifth term calculates the accrued interest agreed to be paid to the seller.

# EXAMPLE

## MEDIUM TERM NOTE

The following example illustrates the calculation of a dollar price for a medium term note given a yield to maturity, with the settlement date in the odd short first coupon period.

| | | |
|---|---|---|
| Settlement Date | | 03/15/93 |
| Maturity Date | | 03/01/20 |
| Issue/Dated Date | | 03/01/93 |
| First coupon date | | 07/01/93 |
| Last Coupon Date | | |
| Before Redemption | | 01/01/20 |
| Day Count Basis | | 30/360 |
| A | = 14 | (03/01/93 - 03/15/93) |
| DFC | = 120 | (03/01/93 - 07/01/93) |
| DLC | = 60 | (01/01/20 - 03/01/20) |
| DSC | = 106 | (03/15/93 - 07/01/93) |
| E | = 180 | (12/15/92 - 06/15/93) |
| M | = 2 | (semi-annual) |
| N | = 54 | (03/15/93 - 01/01/20) |
| NLL | = 180 | (01/01/20 - 07/01/20) |
| R | = 0.04 | (4.00%) |
| RV | = 100 | |
| Y | = 0.0427 | (4.27%) |
| P | = 95.705498 | |
| Dollar Price | = 95.705 | |

# FORMULA 17

[Odd long first and odd short last coupons - Price (given yield)] [Settlement date in odd first period]

$$P = \left[ \frac{RV}{\left(1+\frac{Y}{M}\right)^{N+Nqf+\frac{DSC}{E}+\frac{DLC}{NLL}}} + \frac{100*\frac{R}{M}*\left(\sum\limits_{i=1}^{NCF}\frac{DFC_i}{NLF_i}\right)}{\left(1+\frac{Y}{M}\right)^{Nqf+\frac{DSC}{E}}} + \sum\limits_{K=1}^{N}\frac{100*\frac{R}{M}}{\left(1+\frac{Y}{M}\right)^{K+Nqf+\frac{DSC}{E}}} + \frac{100*\frac{R}{M}*\frac{DLC}{NLL}}{\left(1+\frac{Y}{M}\right)^{N+Nqf+\frac{DSC}{E}+\frac{DLC}{NLL}}} \right] - \left[ 100*\frac{R}{M}*\left(\sum\limits_{i=1}^{NCF}\frac{A_i}{NLF_i}\right) \right]$$

$A_i$ = Number of accrued days for the ith quasi-coupon period within odd period (accrued days)

$DFC_i$ = Number of days from dated date to first quasi-coupon (i=1) or number of days in quasi coupon (i=2,3,...,NCF)

$DLC$ = Number of days from last coupon date before redemption to redemption date

$DSC$ = Number of days from settlement date to first coupon date

$E$ = Number of days in quasi-coupon period in which the settlement date falls

$i$ = A summation counter

$K$ = A summation counter

$M$ = Number of coupon periods per year (standard for the particular security involved)

$N$ = Number of coupons periods between the first real coupon date and last coupon date before redemption (maturity date, call date, put date, etc.)

$NCF$ = Number of quasi-coupon periods that fit in odd first period. (If this number contains a fractional part, raise it to the next whole number - i.e. 2½ = 3)

$NLF_i$ = Normal length in days of the full ith quasi-coupon period within odd first period

$NLL$ = Normal length in days of the full quasi-coupon period in which the odd last period falls

$Nqf$ = Number of whole quasi-coupon periods between settlement date and first coupon (this may be zero)

$P$ = Dollar price per $100 par value

$R$ = Annual interest rate (as a decimal)

$RV$ = Redemption value of the security per $100 par value (RV = 100, except in those cases where call or put features must be considered)

$Y$ = Annual Yield (as a decimal) on investment with security held to redemption

NOTE: The first term calculates present value of the redemption amount, not including interest. The second term calculates the present value of the first coupon payment. The third term calculates present values for all future coupon payments except the first and last coupon payments. The fourth term calculates the present value of the last coupon payment. The fifth term calculates the accrued interest agreed to be paid to the seller.

## MEDIUM TERM NOTE

The following example illustrates the calculation of a dollar price for a medium term note given a yield to maturity, with the settlement date in the odd long first coupon period.

| | | |
|---|---|---|
| Settlement date | | 03/15/93 |
| Maturity date | | 03/01/20 |
| Issue/dated date | | 09/01/92 |
| First coupon date | | 07/01/93 |
| Last Coupon Date | | |
| Before Redemption | | 01/01/20 |
| Day count basis | | 30/360 |
| $A_1$ = | 120 | (09/01/92 - 01/01/93) |
| $A_2$ = | 74 | (01/01/93 - 03/15/93) |
| $DFC_1$ = | 120 | (09/01/92 - 01/01/93) |
| $DFC_2$ = | 180 | (01/01/93 - 07/01/93) |
| DLC = | 60 | (01/01/20 - 03/01/20) |
| DSC = | 106 | (03/15/93 - 07/01/93) |
| E = | 180 | (01/01/93 - 07/01/93) |
| M = | 2 | (semi-annual) |
| N = | 53 | (07/01/93 - 01/01/20) |
| NCF = | 2 | (09/01/92 - 07/01/93) |
| $NLF_1$ = | 180 | (07/01/92 - 01/01/93) |
| $NLF_2$ = | 180 | (01/01/93 - 07/01/93) |
| Nqf = | 0 | (03/15/93 - 07/01/93) |
| R = | 0.046 | (4.6%) |
| RV = | 100 | |
| Y = | 0.1026 | (10.26%) |
| P = | 48.493117 | |
| Dollar Price = | 48.493 | |

# FORMULA 18

[Odd short first and odd long last coupons - Price (given yield)] [Settlement date in odd first period]

$$P = \left[ \frac{RV}{\left(1+\frac{Y}{M}\right)^{N-1+\frac{DSC}{E}+Nq1+\frac{DLQ}{LQL}}} \right] + \left[ \frac{100*\frac{R}{M}*\frac{DFC}{E}}{\left(1+\frac{Y}{M}\right)^{\frac{DSC}{E}}} \right] + \left[ \sum_{K=2}^{N} \frac{100*\frac{R}{M}}{\left(1+\frac{Y}{M}\right)^{K-1+\frac{DSC}{E}}} \right] + \left[ \frac{100*\frac{R}{M}*\left(\sum_{i=1}^{NCL}\frac{DLC_i}{NLL_i}\right)}{\left(1+\frac{Y}{M}\right)^{N-1+\frac{DSC}{E}+Nq1+\frac{DLQ}{LQL}}} \right] - \left[ 100*\frac{R}{M}*\frac{A}{E} \right]$$

$A_i$ = Number of accrued days for the ith quasi-coupon period within odd period (accrued days)

$DFC$ = Number of days from the beginning of the odd first coupon (dated date) to the first coupon date

$DLC_i$ = Number of days from last coupon date before redemption to first quasi-coupon (i=1) or number of days in quasi coupon (i=2,3,...,NCL)

$DLQ$ = Number of days counted in the last ($NCL^{th}$) quasi-coupon period within the odd last period (DLQ = $DLC_i$ where i = NCL)

$DSC$ = Number of days from settlement date to next coupon date

$E$ = Number of days in coupon period in which the settlement date falls

$i$ = A summation counter

$K$ = A summation counter

$LQL$ = Normal length in days of the last ($NCL^{th}$) quasi-coupon period within the odd last period (LQL = $NLL_i$ where i = NCL)

$M$ = Number of coupon periods per year (standard for the particular security involved)

$N$ = Number of coupons periods between settlement date and last coupon date before redemption (maturity date, call date, put date, etc.)

$NCL$ = Number of quasi-coupon periods that fit in odd last period. (If this number contains a fractional part, raise it to the next whole number - i.e. 2½ = 3)

$NLL_i$ = Normal length in days of the full ith quasi-coupon period within odd last period

$Nq1$ = Number of whole quasi-coupon periods between last coupon date before redemption and the redemption date (this may be zero)

$P$ = Dollar price per $100 par value

$R$ = Annual interest rate (as a decimal)

$RV$ = Redemption value of the security per $100 par value (RV = 100, except in those cases where call or put features must be considered)

$Y$ = Annual Yield (as a decimal) on investment with security held to redemption

NOTE: The first term calculates present value of the redemption amount, not including interest. The second term calculates the present value of the first coupon payment. The third term calculates present values for all future coupon payments except the first and last coupon payments. The fourth term calculates the present value of the last coupon payment. The fifth term calculates the accrued interest agreed to be paid to the seller.

100

## MEDIUM TERM NOTE

The following example illustrates the calculation of a dollar price for a medium term note given a yield to maturity, with the settlement date in the odd first period.

| | | |
|---|---|---|
| Settlement date | | 11/22/92 |
| Maturity date | | 12/01/05 |
| Issue/dated date | | 11/01/92 |
| First coupon date | | 01/01/93 |
| Last Interest Date | | |
| Before Redemption | | 01/01/05 |
| Day count basis | | 30/360 |
| $A$ = | 21 | (11/01/92 - 11/22/92) |
| $DFC$ = | 60 | (11/01/92 - 01/01/93) |
| $DLC_1$ = | 180 | (01/01/05 - 07/01/05) |
| $DLC_2$ = | 150 | (07/01/05 - 12/01/05) |
| $DLQ$ = | 150 | (07/01/05 - 12/01/05) |
| $DSC$ = | 39 | (11/22/92 - 01/01/93) |
| $E$ = | 180 | (07/01/92 - 01/01/93) |
| $LQL$ = | 180 | (07/01/05 - 01/01/06) |
| $M$ = | 2 | (semi-annual) |
| $N$ = | 25 | (11/22/92 - 01/01/05) |
| $NCL$ = | 2 | (01/01/05 - 12/01/05) |
| $NLL_1$ = | 180 | (01/01/05 - 07/01/05) |
| $NLL_2$ = | 180 | (07/01/05 - 01/01/06) |
| $Nql$ = | 1 | (01/01/05 - 12/01/05) |
| $R$ = | 0.08 | (8.00%) |
| $RV$ = | 100 | |
| $Y$ = | 0.1101 | (11.01%) |
| $P$ = | 79.401071 | |
| Dollar Price = | 79.401 | |

# FORMULA 19

[Odd long first and odd long last coupon - Price (given yield)] [Settlement date in odd first period]

$$P = \left[\frac{RV}{\left(1+\frac{Y}{M}\right)^{N+Nqf+\frac{DSC}{E}+Nql+\frac{DLQ}{LQL}}}\right] + \left[\frac{100*\frac{R}{M}*\left(\sum_{i=1}^{NCF}\frac{DFC_i}{NLF_i}\right)}{\left(1+\frac{Y}{M}\right)^{Nqf+\frac{DSC}{E}}}\right] + \left[\sum_{K=1}^{N}\frac{100*\frac{R}{M}}{\left(1+\frac{Y}{M}\right)^{K+Nqf+\frac{DSC}{E}}}\right] + \left[\frac{100*\frac{R}{M}*\left(\sum_{i=1}^{NCL}\frac{DLC_i}{NLL_i}\right)}{\left(1+\frac{Y}{M}\right)^{N+Nqf+\frac{DSC}{E}+Nql+\frac{DLQ}{LQL}}}\right] - \left[100*\frac{R}{M}*\left(\sum_{i=1}^{NCF}\frac{A_i}{NLF_i}\right)\right]$$

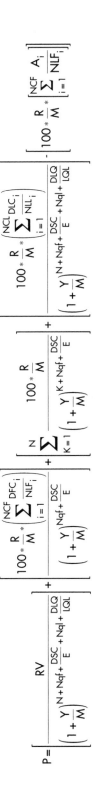

$A_i$ = Number of accrued days for the ith quasi-coupon period within odd period (accrued days)

$DFC_i$ = Number of days from dated date to first quasi-coupon (i=1) or number of days in quasi coupon (i=2,3,...,NCF)

$DLC_i$ = Number of days from last coupon date before redemption to first quasi-coupon (i=1) or number of days in quasi coupon (i=2,3,...,NCL)

$DLQ$ = Number of days counted in the last (NCL)th quasi-coupon period within the odd last period (DLQ = DLC_i where i = NCL)

$DSC$ = Number of days from settlement date - next coupon date

$E$ = Number of days in coupon period in which the settlement date falls

$i$ = A summation counter

$K$ = A summation counter

$LQL$ = Normal length in days of the last (NCL)th quasi-coupon period within the odd last period (LQL = NLL_i where i = NCL)

$M$ = Number of coupon periods per year (standard for the particular security involved)

$N$ = Number of coupons periods between the first real coupon date and last coupon date before redemption (maturity date, call date, put date, etc.)

$NCF$ = Number of quasi-coupon periods that fit in odd first period. (If this number contains a fractional part, raise it to the next whole number - i.e. 2½ = 3)

$NCL$ = Number of quasi-coupon periods that fit in odd last period. (If this number contains a fractional part, raise it to the next whole number - i.e. 2½ = 3)

$NLF_i$ = Normal length in days of the full ith quasi-coupon period within odd first period

$NLL_i$ = Normal length in days of the full ith quasi-coupon period within odd last period

$Nqf$ = Number of whole quasi-coupon periods between settlement date and first coupon (this may be zero)

$Nql$ = Number of whole quasi-coupon periods between last coupon date before redemption and the redemption date (this may be zero)

$P$ = Dollar price per $100 par value

$R$ = Annual interest rate (as a decimal)

$RV$ = Redemption value of the security per $100 par value (RV = 100, except in those cases where call or put features must be considered)

$Y$ = Annual Yield (as a decimal) on investment with security held to redemption

NOTE: The first term calculates present value of the redemption amount, not including interest. The second term calculates the present value of the first coupon payment. The third term calculates present values for all future coupon payments except the first and last coupon payments. The fourth term calculates the present value of the last coupon payment. The fifth term calculates the accrued interest agreed to be paid to the seller.

# EXAMPLE                                    FORMULA 19

## MEDIUM TERM NOTE

The following example illustrates the calculation of a dollar price for a medium term note given a yield to maturity, with the settlement date in the odd first coupon period.

| | | |
|---|---|---|
| Settlement date | | 06/05/92 |
| Maturity date | | 12/15/23 |
| Issue/dated date | | 01/01/92 |
| First coupon date | | 12/15/92 |
| Last Coupon Date | | |
| Before Redemption | | 12/15/22 |
| Day count basis | | 30/360 |
| $A_1$ | = 154 | (01/01/92 - 06/05/92) |
| $A_2$ | = 0 | |
| $DFC_1$ | = 164 | (01/01/92 - 06/15/92) |
| $DFC_2$ | = 180 | (06/15/92 - 12/15/92) |
| $DLC_1$ | = 180 | (12/15/22 - 06/15/23) |
| $DLC_2$ | = 180 | (06/15/23 - 12/15/23) |
| $DLQ$ | = 180 | (06/15/23 - 12/15/23) |
| $DSC$ | = 10 | (06/05/92 - 06/15/92) |
| $E$ | = 180 | (12/15/91 - 06/15/92) |
| $LQL$ | = 180 | (06/15/23 - 12/15/23) |
| $M$ | = 2 | (semi-annual) |
| $N$ | = 60 | (12/15/92 - 12/15/22) |
| $NCF$ | = 2 | (01/01/92 - 12/15/92) |
| $NCL$ | = 2 | (12/15/22 - 12/15/23) |
| $NLF_1$ | = 180 | (12/15/91 - 06/15/92) |
| $NLF_2$ | = 180 | (06/15/92 - 12/15/92) |
| $NLL_1$ | = 180 | (12/15/22 - 06/15/23) |
| $NLL_2$ | = 180 | (06/15/23 - 12/15/23) |
| $Nqf$ | = 1 | (06/05/92 - 12/15/92) |
| $Nql$ | = 2 | (12/15/22 - 12/15/23) |
| $R$ | = 0.05 | (5.00%) |
| $RV$ | = 100 | |
| $Y$ | = 0.0736 | (7.36%) |
| $P$ | = 71.126 | |
| Dollar Price | = 71.126548 | |

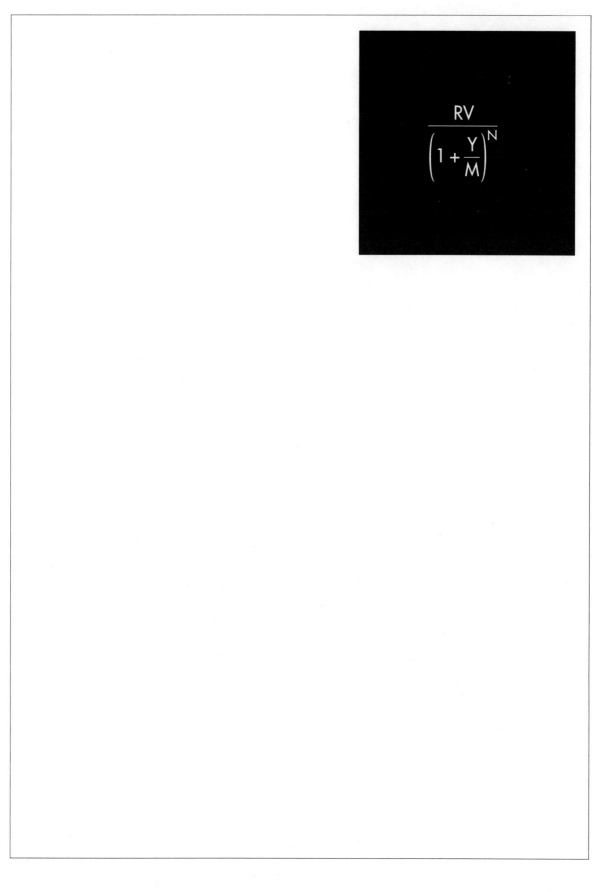

$$\frac{RV}{\left(1 + \dfrac{Y}{M}\right)^{N}}$$

# ZERO COUPON

Securities falling into a pricing category called zero coupon bonds pay no periodic interest. These bonds generally mature more than 1½ years after issue and then pay either principal only or interest and principal.

There are two types of zero coupon bonds: a) **Capital Accretion** and b) **Interest Multiplier**. **Capital Accretion** bonds pay principal (par value) only at maturity to no interest to and are initially sold at a discount to this principal. **Interest Multiplier** bonds pay principal and interest only at maturity and are initially sold around par with interest formulas to compute yield and price. The only difference is the maturity value: for **Capital Accretion** securities, it will be par value and for **Interest Multiplier** it will be par value plus interest.

In comparing Formula 23 with Formula 7, you will notice that the second and third term of Formula 7 are not included in Formula 23. These terms are not included because, since there are no coupons paid, there is no interest rate. $R = 0$. *The coupon is zero.*

In addition to computing price or yield, it is often necessary to calculate the value of a zero coupon security at some point between issue date and maturity date. These intermediate values are called CAV's, Capital Accreted Value or Compound Accreted Value. These values are used for such things as computing accrued interest and call prices. To compute the CAV at any date, substitute in formula 21 or 23 that date for the settlement date and original yield for yield (original yield for a security is that yield at which the security was first issued). The price calculated will be the CAV.

The zero coupon formulas presented are:

| Formula Number | Description |
|---|---|
| 20 | Yield (given price) with one quasi-coupon period or less to redemption |
| 21 | Price (given yield) with one quasi-coupon period or less to redemption |
| 22 | Yield (given price) with more than one quasi-coupon period to redemption |
| 23 | Price (given yield) with more than one quasi-coupon period to redemption |

# Formula 20

[Yield (given price) with one quasi-coupon period or less to redemption]

$$Y = \left[\frac{RV - P}{P}\right] * \left[\frac{M * E}{DSR}\right]$$

DSR = Number of days from settlement date to redemption date (or call date, maturity date, put date, etc.)

E = Number of days in quasi-coupon period

M = Number of quasi-coupon periods per year (standard for the particular security involved)

P = Dollar price per $100 par value

RV = Redemption value per $100 par value

Y = Annual Yield (as a decimal) on investment with security held to redemption

NOTE: The first term calculates yield on invested dollars. The second term converts this yield to a per annum basis.

NOTE: Quasi-coupon periods are the coupon periods which would exist if the bond was paying interest at a rate other than zero.

# EXAMPLE

## MUNICIPAL BOND

The following example illustrates the calculation of a yield given dollar price for a municipal zero coupon bond with less than one quasi-coupon to redemption.

| | | |
|---|---|---|
| Settlement Date | | 06/23/92 |
| Maturity Date | | 10/01/92 |
| Day Count Basis | | 30/360 |
| DSR | = 98 | (06/23/92 - 10/01/92) |
| E | = 180 | (04/01/92 - 10/01/92) |
| P | = 98.875 | ($98.875) |
| M | = 2 | (quasi semi-annual) |
| RV | = 100.000 | |
| Y | = 0.04179674 | |
| Yield | = 4.180 | |

# FORMULA 21

[Price (given yield) with one quasi-coupon period or less to redemption]

$$P = \left[ \frac{RV}{1 + \left( \dfrac{DSR}{E} * \dfrac{Y}{M} \right)} \right]$$

DSR = Number of days from settlement date to redemption date (call date, maturity date, put date, etc.)

E = Number of days in quasi-coupon period

M = Number of quasi-coupon periods per year (standard for the particular security involved)

P = Dollar price per $100 par value

RV = Redemption value of the security per $100 maturity value (RV = 100, except in those cases where call or put features must be considered)

Y = Annual Yield (as a decimal) on investment with security held to redemption

NOTE: Quasi-coupon periods are the coupon periods which would exist if the bond was paying interest at a rate other than zero.

# EXAMPLE

## MUNICIPAL BOND

The following example illustrates the calculation of a dollar price given a yield for a municipal zero coupon bond with one or less quasi-coupon period to redemption.

| | | |
|---|---|---|
| Settlement Date | 08/15/92 | |
| Maturity Date | 10/01/92 | |
| Day Count Basis | 30/360 | |
| DSR = 46 | (08/15/92 - 10/01/92) |
| E = 180 | (04/01/92 - 10/01/92) |
| M = 2 | (quasi semi-annual) |
| RV = 100.000 | |
| Y = 0.0625 | (6¼%) |
| P = 99.207716 | |
| Dollar Price = 99.207 | |

# Formula 22

[Yield (given price) with more than one quasi-coupon period to redemption]

$$Y = \left[ \left( \frac{RV}{P} \right)^{\left( \frac{1}{Nq - 1 + \frac{DSC}{E}} \right)} - 1 \right] * M$$

DSC = Number of days from settlement date to the next quasi-coupon date as if the security paid periodic interest

E = Numbers of days in quasi-coupon period in which settlement date falls

M = Number of quasi-coupon periods per year (standard for the particular security involved)

Nq = Number of quasi-coupon periods between settlement date and redemption date (if this number contains a fractional part, raise it to the next whole number - i.e. 2½ = 3)

P = Dollar price per $100 par value

RV = Redemption value of the security per $100 maturity value (RV = 100, except in those cases where call or put features must be considered)

Y = Annual yield (as a decimal) on investment with security held to redemption

NOTE: Quasi-coupon periods are the coupon periods which would exist if the bond was paying interest at a rate other than zero.

# EXAMPLE

## CORPORATE BOND

The following example illustrates the calculation of a yield given a dollar price for a corporate zero coupon bond with more than one quasi-coupon to redemption.

| | | |
|---|---|---|
| Settlement Date | | 06/26/92 |
| Maturity Date | | 07/01/05 |
| Day Count Basis | | 30/360 |
| DSC | = 5 | (06/26/92 - 07/01/92) |
| E | = 180 | (01/01/92 - 07/01/92) |
| M | = 2 | (quasi semi-annual) |
| Nq | = 27 | (06/26/92 - 07/01/05) |
| RV | = 100.000 | |
| P | = 25.125 | ($25.125) |
| Y | = 0.10900794 | |
| Yield | = 10.900794 | |

# Formula 23

[Price (given yield) with more than one quasi-coupon period to redemption]

$$P = \left[ \frac{RV}{\left(1 + \dfrac{Y}{M}\right)^{Nq - 1 + \frac{DSC}{E}}} \right]$$

DSC = Number of days from settlement date to the next quasi-coupon date as if the security paid periodic interest

E = Numbers of days in quasi-coupon period

M = Number of quasi-coupon periods per year (standard for the particular security involved)

Nq = Number of quasi-coupon periods between settlement date and redemption date (if this number contains a fractional part, raise it to the next whole number to i.e. 2½ = 3)

P = Dollar price per $100 par value

RV = Redemption value of the security per $100 par value (RV = 100, except in those cases where call or put features must be considered)

Y = Annual yield (as a decimal) on investment with security held to redemption

NOTE: Quasi-coupon periods are the coupon periods which would exist if the bond was paying interest at a rate other than zero.

# EXAMPLE                                              FORMULA 23

## MUNICIPAL BOND

The following example illustrates the calculation of a dollar price given a yield for a municipal bond with more than one quasi-coupon to redemption.

| | | |
|---|---|---|
| Settlement Date | 02/12/92 | |
| Maturity Date | 07/01/05 | |
| Day Count Basis | 30/360 | |
| DSC = 139 | (02/12/92 - 07/01/92) | |
| E = 180 | (01/01/92 - 07/01/92) | |
| M = 2 | (quasi semi-annual) | |
| Nq = 27 | (02/12/92 - 07/01/05) | |
| RV = 100.000 | | |
| Y = 0.1055 | (10.55%) | |
| P = 25.252446 | | |
| Dollar Price = 25.252 | | |

115

$$\sum_{K_2=1}^{N_2} \frac{100 * \frac{R_2}{M}}{\left(1 + \frac{Y}{M}\right)^{K_2 - 1 + \frac{DSC}{E}}}$$

## STEPPED COUPONS

In addition to securities with one coupon rate which pay interest on a periodic payment schedule, there are periodic payment securities which change the coupon rate after the first few years. For example, for the first 10 years, a security may have a coupon of 5.50% and for the second 10 years a coupon of 7.30%, or 0% for the first 5 years and 7.30% for the next 25 years. These securities have been called Stepped Coupon securities because the coupon rates are fixed (unlike variable rate bonds), and generally the coupon rate "steps" up after a set number of payment periods. As long as the coupons are fixed and the number of payment periods each coupon pays is known, the price and yield can be computed.

Unlike Stepped Coupon securities, the price and yield for variable rate securities cannot be computed because not all the coupon rates are known.

On the following pages are two formulas for computing price when given yield. The first, 24, is for securities which have no coupons for the first few years and then "convert" to a regular coupon paying security. This generally is done on a month and day "in sync" with the maturity date. Formula 24, to compute the price, given the yield of these securities is a combination of both Formula 7 and Formula 22.

The other type of Stepped Coupon considered pays coupon interest at one rate and then "converts" to another rate. The formula, Formula 25, is an expansion of Formula 7, which splits "N," the number of coupons from settlement to redemption, into two factors, "$N_1$," the number of coupons from settlement to conversion date, and "$N_2$," the number of coupons from conversion date to redemption date. This can be further expanded to any number of "steps" as long as the proper interest rate is kept with the correct interest periods.

The Stepped Coupon Formulas are:

| Formula Number | Description |
|---|---|
| 24* | Price (given yield) for stepped coupon securities with "zero" coupon first. |
| 25* | Price (given yield) for stepped coupon securities with interest paid in each "step" |

---

*For "yield given price" calculations, a method of iteration must be used (see section "Iteration Theory and Solving for Yield").

# FORMULA 24

[Price (given yield) for Stepped Coupons with zero coupon first]

$$P = \left[ \frac{1}{\left(1 + \dfrac{Y}{M}\right)^{Nq - 1 + \frac{DSC}{E}}} \right] * \left[ \frac{RV}{\left(1 + \dfrac{Y}{M}\right)^{N}} + \sum_{K=1}^{N} \frac{100 * \dfrac{R}{M}}{\left(1 + \dfrac{Y}{M}\right)^{K}} \right]$$

DSC = Number of days from settlement date to next quasi-coupon date

E = Numbers of days in quasi-coupon period in which the settlement date falls

K = A summation counter

M = Number of coupon periods per year (standard for the particular security involved)

Nq = Number of quasi-coupon periods between settlement date and conversion date (if this number contains a fractional part, raise it to the next whole number - i.e. 2½ = 3)

N = Number of coupon periods between the conversion date and redemption date

P = Dollar price per $100 par value

RV = Redemption value of the security per $100 par value (RV = 100 except in those cases where call or put features must be considered)

Y = Annual yield (as a decimal) on investment with security held to redemption

NOTE: The first term (when multiplied times the second term) calculates the present value of the periodic payment and zero coupon parts of the security. The first part in the second term calculates the present value of the redemption amount for the periodic payment part of the security. The second part in the second term calculates present values for all coupon payments in the periodic payment part of the security.

Actual Data for run date ? ?

Maturity: 5-1-05   Issue: 5-1-91

Coupon steps (accrues new rate)

starting 5-1-99, so 11-1-99

is first coupon at new rate. 5-1-99

is coupon date [15].

## MUNICIPAL BOND

The following example illustrates the calculation of a dollar price given a yield for a Municipal Stepped Coupon Bond with zero coupon first.

| | | |
|---|---|---|
| Settlement Date | 03/16/92 | |
| Maturity Date | 05/01/93 | |
| Conversion Coupon | 8⅞% | |
| Maturity Date | 05/01/99 | |
| Day Count Basis | 30/360 | |
| DSC = 45 | (03/16/92 - 05/01/92) | |
| E = 180 | (11/01/91 - 05/01/92) | |
| Nq = 15 | (03/16/92 - 05/01/99) | |
| N = 12 | (05/01/99 - 05/01/99) | |
| R = 0.08875 | (8⅞%) | |
| RV = 100 | | |
| Y = 0.09305 | (9.305%) | |
| P = 51.291390 | | |
| Dollar Price = 51.291 | | |

# FORMULA 25

[Price (given yield) with two non-zero coupon steps]

$$P = \left[\dfrac{1}{\left(1+\dfrac{Y}{M}\right)^{N_1-1+\frac{DSC}{E}}}\right] * \left[\dfrac{RV}{\left(1+\dfrac{Y}{M}\right)^{N_2}} + \sum_{K_2=1}^{N_2}\dfrac{100*\dfrac{R_2}{M}}{\left(1+\dfrac{Y}{M}\right)^{K_2}}\right] + \left[\sum_{K_1=1}^{N_1}\dfrac{100*\dfrac{R_1}{M}}{\left(1+\dfrac{Y}{M}\right)^{K_1-1+\frac{DSC}{E}}}\right] - \left[100*\dfrac{R_1}{M}*\dfrac{A}{E}\right]$$

- A = Number of days from beginning of coupon period to settlement date (accrued days)

- DSC = Number of days from settlement date to next coupon date

- E = Numbers of days in coupon period in which the settlement date falls

- $K_1$ = A summation counter

- $K_2$ = A summation counter

- M = Number of coupon periods per year (standard for the particular security involved)

- $N_1$ = Number of coupon periods between settlement date and conversion date (if this number contains a fractional part, raise it to the next whole number - i.e. 2½ = 3)

- $N_2$ = Number of coupon periods between the conversion date and redemption date

- P = Dollar price per $100 par value

- $R_1$ = Annual interest rate (as a decimal) from settlement date to conversion date

- $R_2$ = Annual interest rate (as a decimal) from conversion date to redemption date

- RV = Redemption value of the security per $100 par value (RV = 100 except in those cases where call or put features must be considered)

- Y = Annual yield (as a decimal) on investment with security held to redemption

NOTE: The first term (when multiplied times the second term) calculates the present value of the redemption value and the coupon payments from conversion date to redemption date. The second term calculates the present value of the redemption value and coupon payments from conversion date to redemption. The third term calculates present values for all coupon payments from settlement date to conversion date. The fourth term calculates the accrued interest agreed to be paid to the seller.

# EXAMPLE

# FORMULA 25

## MUNICIPAL BOND

The following example illustrates the calculation of a dollar price given a yield for a municipal stepped coupon bond.

| | | |
|---|---|---|
| Settlement Date | 08/02/92 | |
| Coupon | 7½% | |
| Conversion Date | 12/15/03 | |
| Conversion Coupon | 8⅞% | |
| Maturity Date | 06/15/10 | |
| Day Count Basis | 30/360 | |
| $A$ = 47 | (06/15/92 - 08/02/92) | |
| $DSC$ = 133 | (08/02/92 - 12/15/92) | |
| $E$ = 180 | (06/15/92 - 12/15/92) | |
| $N_1$ = 23 | (08/02/92 - 12/15/03) | |
| $N_2$ = 13 | (12/15/03 - 06/15/10) | |
| $R_1$ = 0.07500 | (7½%) | |
| $R_2$ = 0.08875 | (8⅞%) | |
| $RV$ = 100 | | |
| $Y$ = 0.07221 | (7.221%) | |
| $P$ = 105.903371 | | |
| Dollar Price = 105.903 | | |

*Handwritten margin notes:*

Actual Dates

Mat: 6/15/10    Issue: 6/15/92

[P123]

Coupon steps (accrues new rate) as of 12/15/03, which is Coupon Date [22].

First coupon at new rate is coupon 23 (from 0).

123

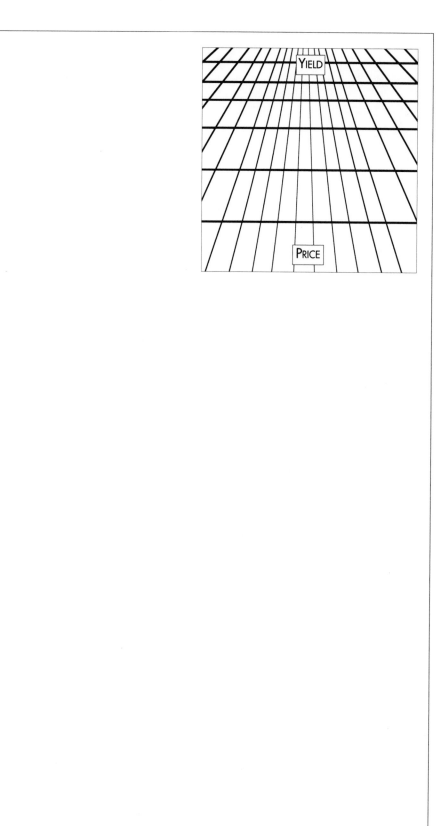

Gary Bronson, Ph.d. and Richard Bronson, Ph.d.

## ITERATION THEORY

Unlike the equations for determining a bond's price from its yield to maturity, no simple formula exists for calculating a bond's yield to maturity given its price. First the reason for this and the mathematical basis ensuring the existence of a unique yield to maturity are presented. Then specific calculation techniques to solve for yield are given.

The yield to maturity takes into account the time value of money; it is the interest rate that discounts the stream of coupons and final bond redemption value back to the agreed upon price. Assuming the valuation date falls on an interest payment date (that is, ignoring accrued interest), the price of a bond is

$$P \ = \ \frac{C}{M} * \left(1 + \frac{Y}{M}\right)^{-1} + \frac{C}{M} * \left(1 + \frac{Y}{M}\right)^{-2} + \ldots + \frac{C}{M} * \left(1 + \frac{Y}{M}\right)^{-N} + RV * \left(1 + \frac{Y}{M}\right)^{-N}$$

EQUATION (1)

where:

| | | |
|---|---|---|
| P | = | bond price, in dollars |
| C | = | annual coupon payment, in dollars |
| RV | = | redemption value, in dollars |
| Y | = | yield to maturity, as a decimal rate |
| N | = | total number of remaining periods |
| M | = | number of coupon periods per year |

Equation (1) is, of course, the basis for the standard bond pricing formula, given as Formula 7 (page 66). We now show that Equation (1) has a unique non-zero yield solution which must be positive for all problems of practical value. Once we are guaranteed that this is true, specific techniques for obtaining the unique yield solution are presented.

For notational simplicity, we set $x = 1 + Y/M$ and $q = C/(M*P)$. Then Equation (1) can be rewritten as

$$1 \ = \ q * x^{-1} + q * x^{-2} + \ldots + q * x^{-N} + \frac{RV}{P} * x^{-N}$$

Multiplying both sides of this equation by $x^N$ and bringing all terms over to the left-side of the equation yields:

$$x^N - q * \left(x^{N-1} + x^{N-2} + \ldots + 1\right) - \frac{RV}{P} \ = \ 0$$

EQUATION (2)

127

The terms within the parentheses represent the sum of a geometric series. It is known from algebra that the sum of this series is

$$\frac{1 - x^N}{1 - x}$$

Therefore, Equation (2) may be expressed in the closed form

$$x^N - q * \left(\frac{1 - x^N}{1 - x}\right) - \frac{RV}{P} = 0$$

Multiplying both sides of this last equation by (1 - x) and rearranging terms, we obtain

$$x^{(N + 1)} - (1 + q) * x^N - \left(\frac{RV}{P}\right) * x + \left(q + \frac{RV}{P}\right) = 0$$

EQUATION (3)

where

$$x = 1 + \frac{Y}{M} \quad \text{and} \quad q = \frac{C}{(M * P)}$$

Equation (3) is a polynomial equation of degree N+1 in the variable x. From algebra it is known that every polynomial of degree N+1 has N+1 roots. By a root, of course, we mean a value of x such that the left-side of the equation evaluates to zero. Unfortunately, these N+1 roots can be either positive, negative, or complex. Additionally, general formulas for obtaining these roots do not exist when the number of roots is greater than four.

Equation (3) is one degree higher than Equation (2) as a direct result of multiplying the latter by the term (1 - x). Thus, Equation (3) has one more root that Equation (2), and, not surprisingly, this additional root is x = 1, the value of x that makes the common factor (1 - x) disappear. The important point is that except for the additional root x = 1, the roots of Equation (3) and Equation (2) are identical.

For our purposes the only roots to Equation (3) of practical interest are positive values of x greater than unity. This is because the yield to maturity, Y, is related to the variable x by the equation x = 1 + Y / M. Thus, for the yield to be greater than zero, x must be greater than unity.

An principal of algebra is Descartes' Rule of Signs which states, among other things, that the number of positive real roots of an nth order polynomial with a non-zero constant term cannot exceed the number of coefficient sign changes displayed by the polynomial. Since the constant term in Equation (3) is (q + RV / P) which can never be zero, Descartes' Rule applies. As this equation has two coefficient sign changes ( + to - and then - to + ), we are assured that the equation has either two, one, or no roots.

Descartes' Rule of Signs additionally states that the difference between the number of coefficient sign changes and the number of positive roots must be an even integer. Since our equation has two sign changes it can either have two or no roots, as a single root would yield an odd integer when subtracted from the number of sign changes. But we already know one root to Equation (3) is x = 1. This known root rules out the possibility of the equation having no roots and leaves the remaining possibility of exactly two positive roots.

If we were assured that the second positive root of Equation (3) satisfies the constraint x > 1, we would know that this second root always provides a positive yield greater than zero. To ascertain when this is the case, we calculate the slope at x = 1 of the function whose roots are determined by Equation (3).

Setting

$$p(x) = x^{N+1} - (1+q) * x^N - \left(\frac{RV}{P}\right) * x + \left(q + \frac{RV}{P}\right)$$

which is simply the left side of Equation (3), and taking the derivative of p(x) yields

$$p'(x) = (N+1) * x^N - N * (1+q) * x^{N-1} - \frac{RV}{P}$$

At the root x = 1, the derivative has the value

$$p'(1) = 1 - N * q - \frac{RV}{P}$$

EQUATION 4

There are three cases to consider. The first, which is the most interesting because it is the only one of practical value, occurs when the sum of the coupon stream and the principle repayment is greater than the bond price. In this case,

$$P < N * \left(\frac{C}{M}\right) + RV$$

129

Dividing by P and recalling that q = C / (M*P), we have that

$$1 < N * q + \frac{RV}{P}$$

or

$$1 - N * q - \frac{RV}{P} < 0$$

It then follows from Equation (4) that the function p(x) has a negative slope at the positive root x = 1. Combining this slope information with our previous knowledge of p(x) and also noting that p(x) is always positive for large values of x, we can sketch part of the graph of p(x). This is done in Figure 1.

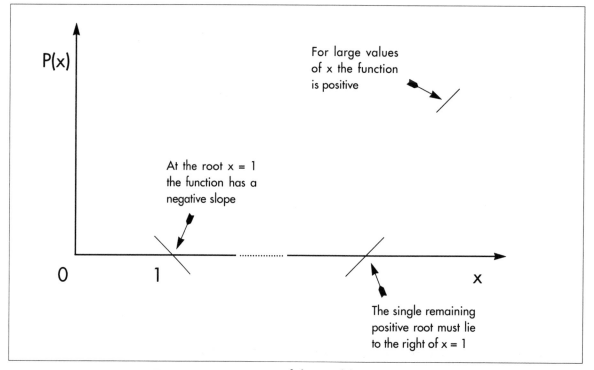

Figure 1 - Structure of the Yield Function P(x)

Figure 1 reflects that

1.  At x = 1 the value of p(x) is zero.
2.  Due to the negative slope at the root x = 1, the curve crosses from a positive functional value to a negative functional value at this root.
3.  The function p(x) is positive for large values of x.
4.  The function p(x) has exactly two positive roots.

130

Notice that since the slope of p(x) is negative at the root x = 1, the function must take on negative values immediately to the right of this root. However, as shown in Figure 1, the function becomes positive for larger values of x. Additionally, we know that only one more positive root exists. Therefore, this remaining zero crossing must lie to the right of the point x = 1, which allows the curve to become positive for larger values of x.

Having determined that the second root has a value greater than one ensures that the yield corresponding to this root will have a positive value greater than zero. Knowing that such a unique positive yield always exists, the problem now is to find it. We show how below.

The two other cases relating P, N, C, and RV are of no practical importance and are mentioned here only for mathematical completeness. If the bond price was equal to the sum of all future coupon payments and redemption value (i.e. P = N*(C/M) + RV), then the yield to maturity must be zero for Equation (3) to be satisfied. Finally, a price greater than the coupon stream plus redemption value (i.e. P > N*(C/M) + RV) means that the net present value of the stream of all payments is greater than the face value of the stream. In this case the derivative in Equation (4) is positive. Using similar reasoning to that which produced Figure 1 shows that the second positive root of p(x) occurs between zero and unity, which corresponds to a negative yield to maturity. These later two pricing alternatives, although mathematically defined, do not occur in practice.

## Solving for Yield

Having shown that for any given price, P, Equation (1) has a unique non-zero solution for Yield (Y), we now describe various techniques for finding the unique yield solution to Equation (1) and comment on their relative efficiencies.

To reiterate, the yield to maturity is the interest rate that discounts the stream of coupons and final bond redemption value back to the agreed upon price. Assuming the valuation date falls on an interest payment date (that is, ignoring accrued interest) the price of a bond is

$$P = \frac{C}{M} * \left(1 + \frac{Y}{M}\right)^{-1} + \frac{C}{M} * \left(1 + \frac{Y}{M}\right)^{-2} + \ldots + \frac{C}{M} * \left(1 + \frac{Y}{M}\right)^{-N} + RV * \left(1 + \frac{Y}{M}\right)^{-N}$$

EQUATION (1) from page # 127

where:

| | | |
|---|---|---|
| P | = | bond price, in dollars |
| C | = | annual coupon payment, in dollars |
| RV | = | redemption value, in dollars |
| Y | = | yield to maturity, as a decimal rate |
| N | = | total number of remaining periods |
| M | = | number of coupon periods per year |

For computational purposes, we subtract the price, P, from the right hand side of the equation and rewrite Equation (1) as

$$F(Y) = \frac{C}{M} * \left(1 + \frac{Y}{M}\right)^{-1} + \frac{C}{M} * \left(1 + \frac{Y}{M}\right)^{-2} + \cdots + \frac{C}{M} * \left(1 + \frac{Y}{M}\right)^{-N} + RV * \left(1 + \frac{Y}{M}\right)^{-N} - P$$

EQUATION (5)

which can be simplified (see Page 139) to:

$$F(Y) = \frac{C}{Y} * \left[1 - \left(1 + \frac{Y}{M}\right)^{-N}\right] + RV * \left(1 + \frac{Y}{M}\right)^{-N} - P$$

EQUATION (6)

Solving Equation (1) for the yield that makes the equation's right side equal the price, P, is the same as solving Equation (6) for the yield that makes F(Y) equal to zero. Such a value of Y is called a root of the equation. From the first part of this article we are assured that one and only one valid root exists.

For maturities of less than two remaining periods (N = 1 or N = 2), Equation (6) reduces to either a linear or quadratic equation, which may be solved algebraically in a straightforward manner. For larger values of N no closed formula exists for determining the roots of Equation (6), and other techniques must be used to locate the root.

The general procedure for determining the root of Equation (6), as in all root finding methods, depends on selecting an initial approximation for the yield and then sequentially modifying the approximation until F(Y) becomes zero. In practice the initial approximation is usually taken as a typical coupon rate, and the iterations continue until one reaches the required degree of accuracy. For financial calculations, all calculations are performed in double precision to at least ten decimal places with the result rounded or truncated according to industry standards.

**Fixed-Increment Method**

The fixed-increment method, although rarely used in practice, is instructive in understanding the underlying basis of all other root-finding methods. As such, this technique is worth explaining.

In fixed-increment root-finding, each yield value, Y, is obtained from the previous approximation by adding or subtracting a fixed amount. To understand how this procedure works in practice, consider a semiannual payment 8% coupon bond with five years to maturity offered at a price of 79.69. For this bond, the equivalent price equation is:

$$796.9 = 40 * \left(1 + \frac{Y}{M}\right)^{-1} + 40 * \left(1 + \frac{Y}{M}\right)^{-2} + \cdots + 40 * \left(1 + \frac{Y}{M}\right)^{-10} + 1000 * \left(1 + \frac{Y}{M}\right)^{-10}$$

EQUATION (7)

Rewriting Equation (7) in the form of Equation (6) results in:

$$F(Y) = \frac{80}{Y} * \left[ 1 - \left(1 + \frac{Y}{M}\right)^{-10} \right] + RV * \left(1 + \frac{Y}{M}\right)^{-10} - 796.9$$

EQUATION (8)

Determining the yield that provides a price of 79.69 now becomes equivalent to finding a value of Y that makes F(Y) in Equation (8) equal to zero.

In fixed increment root finding, as in all root finding methods, an initial yield approximation is selected and Equation (7) evaluated. If the initial approximation results in a positive value for F(Y), the yield is too low and a fixed amount is added to each approximation until the F(Y) goes negative. Similarly, if the initial yield value results in a negative value for F(Y), the initial approximation of the yield is too high and a fixed increment is subtracted from each successive yield value until F(Y) goes positive. Once the value of F(Y) switches sign, the final approximation to the root is obtained by interpolating between the two values of yield that caused the sign switch.

For example, arbitrarily starting at a yield of 8% and using a fixed increment of 0.0000000001 to determine the root of Equation (8) requires over one hundred million iterations to locate the two values of yield that cause the sign of F(Y) to change. Table 1 lists the values of Yield and F(Y) for the four iterations immediately before and at the sign change. Interpolating between the yield values 0.1375000275 and 0.1375000276 for which F(Y) changes sign, and rounding to six decimal places, results in the value 0.137500 as the calculated yield.

| Yield | F(Y) |
|-------|------|
| 0.1375000272 | 0.0000009520 |
| 0.1375000273 | 0.0000006459 |
| 0.1375000274 | 0.0000003398 |
| 0.1375000275 | 0.0000000336 |
| 0.1375000276 | - 0.0000002725 |

## Bisection Method

The bisection method is a straightforward and simple-to-program technique that typically converges much quicker than the fixed increment method. It differs from the fixed increment method in that two initial approximations are required for the Yield, one that makes F(Y) in Equation (3) positive and a second that makes F(Y) negative. Generally, the typical coupon rate is taken as one approximation. If that rate generates a positive value for F(Y), then the second approximation is typically taken six-hundred basis points higher. If F(Y) is negative for the typical coupon rate, then the second approximation is initially taken as six-hundred basis points lower. Six hundred basis points is almost always sufficient; in the rare case it is not, a larger increment should be taken. Thus, it is easy to identify two points a and b, one of which is the typical coupon rate, such that F(a) > 0 and F(b) < 0. It follows from Figure 2-A that the root of F(Y) lies between a and b.

In the bisection method the midpoint of the initial two yield values is calculated and used to replace either a or b.  The midpoint value is determined as:

$$mid = (a+b) / 2.0$$

The value F(mid) is then calculated. If the sign of F(mid) is the same as the sign of F(a), a is replaced by mid, else b is replaced by mid, and a new midpoint is calculated. In either case the root remains in the new interval. For example, in Figure 2-A, the sign of F(mid) is the same as F(b). As illustrated, this corresponds to the point Y = mid being to the right of the root Yr and requires replacing the value of  b with mid in the next calculation.

The second calculation of mid uses the new value of b and results in a value to the left of the root, as illustrated in Figure 2-B. Here F(mid) has the same sign as F(a), which means that in the next calculation the value of a is replaced by the value of mid. As indicated by Figures 2-A and 2-B, each calculation of a new midpoint results in reducing the initial interval between Y = a and Y = b by a factor of two, or in other words bisecting the remaining interval. If an initial interval is selected that is known to contain the yield, the method will always converge. With this as background, the bisection algorithm is as follows:

> Select a lower and higher yield bound that contains the root
>
> Repeat the following until F(Y) is within 10-10  of zero
>
>> Calculate the midpoint of the current interval
>> If F(Y) at the left bound and at the midpoint have the same sign
>> then
>>> Make the new left bound the midpoint value
>> else
>>> Make the new right bound the midpoint value

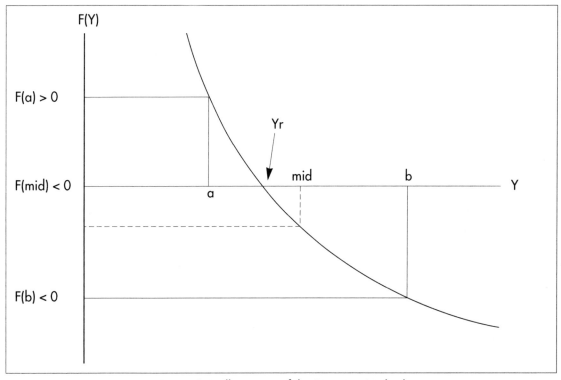

Figure 2-A  Illustration of the Bisection Method

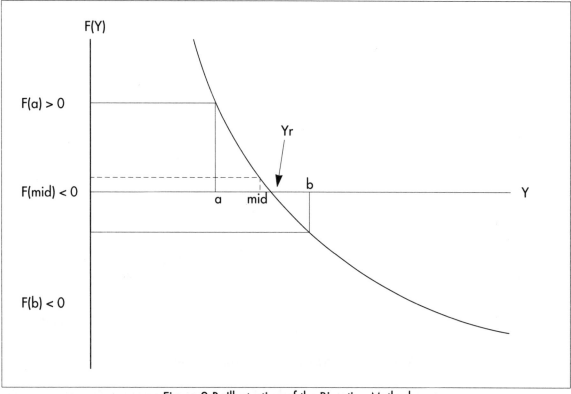

Figure 2-B  Illustration of the Bisection Method

Using the bisection method on our previous example (price = 79.69, coupon = .08, five years to maturity) with initial bounds of .08 and .14 resulted in a root of .137500 in 41 iterations.

**False Position Method**

The method of false position is a variation of the bisection method that is initialized the same way, with two points a and b having the properties that F(a) > 0 and F(b) < 0. Now, however, a chord is drawn between the two points (a, F(a)) and (b, F(b)) as illustrated in Figure 3, and the point of intersection c between this chord and the Yield axis is determined. This point c serves the same purpose as the point mid in the bisection method. If F(c) > 0, then c replaces a. If F(c) < 0, then c replaces b. In either case, once the substitution is made, the iteration continues anew.

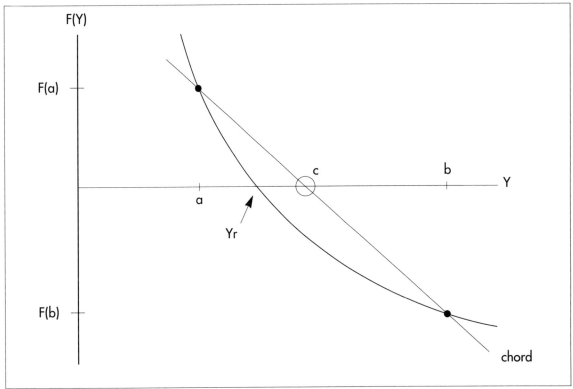

Figure 3   Illustration of the False-Position Method

The equation of a chord illustrated in Figure 3 is simply the equation of a straight line through two known points. Its point of intersection with the Yield axis is given algebraically by:

$$c = a + \frac{F(a)}{F(a) - F(b)} * (b - a)$$

EQUATION (9)

The method of false position is no more efficient in locating roots than the bisection method and, because it is more complicated to use, this technique is rarely employed.  Surprisingly, however, a slight modification produces a method that is significantly quicker than any of the previous ones.

## Secant Method

The secant method is identical to the method of false position except that the sign of F(Y) need not be checked at each iteration. As in the method of false position, the values of a and b are required to start the procedure and Equation (5) is used to calculate c. But then, we simply replace a with b (that is, b becomes a), replace b with c (that is, c becomes the new b), and return to Equation (5) to generate the new c. This procedure continues until F(c) is within 10-10 of zero; whereupon the value of c is taken as the desired Yield to maturity.

Employing the secant method on our previous example (price = 79.69, coupon = .08, five years to maturity) with initial bounds of a = .08 and b =.14 (the same initial approximations used in the Bisection method) resulted in a root of .137500 in 4 iterations. This compares to the 41 iterations required using the Bisection method. Additionally, it should be noted that the secant method, unlike the bisection method, does not require that the two initial yield approximations encompass the actual root.

## Newton-Raphson Method

The most efficient of all commonly used root-finding methods is the Newton-Raphson method. In contrast to the bisection method, the method of false position, and the secant method, all of which require two points to initialize them, the Newton-Raphson method, like the fixed-point method, requires only a single initial approximation to generate the next approximation.

The Newton-Raphson method is illustrated in Figure 4 (on the next page). A line is constructed through the point (a, F(a)) having the same slope as the curve at this point (that is, a tangent line is constructed). The point of intersection between the tangent line and the Yield-axis becomes the next approximation for the root. Since the slope of the tangent line is the derivative of the function, the Newton-Raphson method is a calculus based method requiring that the derivative of F(Y) be known. For the Price/Yield Equation of a bond described by Equation (3), this derivative can always be taken and is shown on page 139 to be:

$$F'(Y) = -\frac{C}{Y^2} + \left(1 + \frac{Y}{M}\right)^{-N-1} * \left[\frac{C}{Y^2} + \frac{C*(1+N)}{M*Y} - \frac{N*RV}{M}\right]$$

EQUATION (10)

Designating the current approximation to the root as $Y_i$ and the next approximation as $Y_{i+1}$ and using the derivative information, the Newton-Raphson method produces the formula:

$$Y_{i+1} = Y_i - F(Y_i) / F'(Y_i)$$

In almost all cases the Newton-Raphson Method converges to the actual root quicker than any of the non-calculus based root-finding methods.

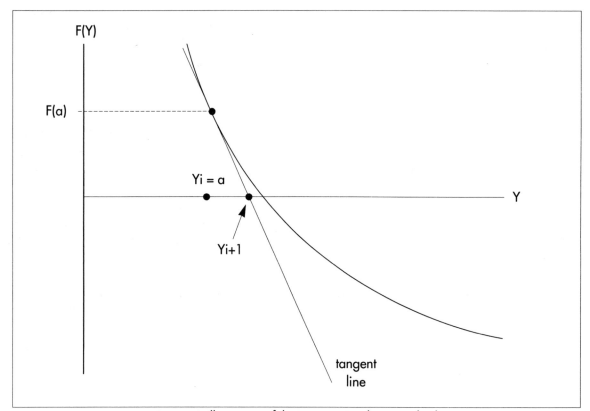

Figure 4  Illustration of the Newton-Raphson Method

# Derivation of Equation (6)

Starting with Equation (5) we have:

$$F(Y) = \frac{C}{M}*\left(1+\frac{Y}{M}\right)^{-1} + \frac{C}{M}*\left(1+\frac{Y}{M}\right)^{-2} + \cdots + \frac{C}{M}*\left(1+\frac{Y}{M}\right)^{-N} + RV*\left(1+\frac{Y}{M}\right)^{-N} - P$$

$$= \frac{C}{M}*\left(1+\frac{Y}{M}\right)^{-1}*\left[1+\left(1+\frac{Y}{M}\right)^{-1} + \cdots + \left(1+\frac{Y}{M}\right)^{-(N-1)}\right] + RV*\left(1+\frac{Y}{M}\right)^{-N} - P$$

$$= \frac{C}{M}*\left(1+\frac{Y}{M}\right)^{-1}*\frac{\left[1-\left(1+\frac{Y}{M}\right)^{-N}\right]}{\left[1-\left(1+\frac{Y}{M}\right)^{-1}\right]} + RV*\left(1+\frac{Y}{M}\right)^{-N} - P$$

$$= \frac{C}{M}*\left(1+\frac{Y}{M}\right)^{-1}*\frac{\left[1-\left(1+\frac{Y}{M}\right)^{-N}\right]}{\left(\frac{Y}{M}\right)*\left(1+\frac{Y}{M}\right)^{-1}} + RV*\left(1+\frac{Y}{M}\right)^{-N} - P$$

$$= \frac{C}{Y}*\left[1-\left(1+\frac{Y}{M}\right)^{-N}\right] + RV*\left(1+\frac{Y}{M}\right)^{-N} - P$$

# Derivation of Equation (10)

Taking the derivative of Equation (6), term-by-term, yields:

$$F'(Y) = -\frac{C}{Y^2}*\left[1-\left(1+\frac{Y}{M}\right)^{-N}\right] + \frac{C}{Y}*\left[\frac{N}{M}*\left(1+\frac{Y}{M}\right)^{-N-1}\right] - \frac{N*RV}{M}*\left(1+\frac{Y}{M}\right)^{-N-1}$$

$$= -\frac{C}{Y^2} + \left(1+\frac{Y}{M}\right)^{-N-1}*\left[\frac{C}{Y^2}*\left(1+\frac{Y}{M}\right) + \frac{C*N}{M*Y} - \frac{N*RV}{M}\right]$$

$$= -\frac{C}{Y^2} + \left(1+\frac{Y}{M}\right)^{-N-1}*\left[\frac{C}{Y^2} + \frac{C}{M*Y}*(1+N) - \frac{N*RV}{M}\right]$$

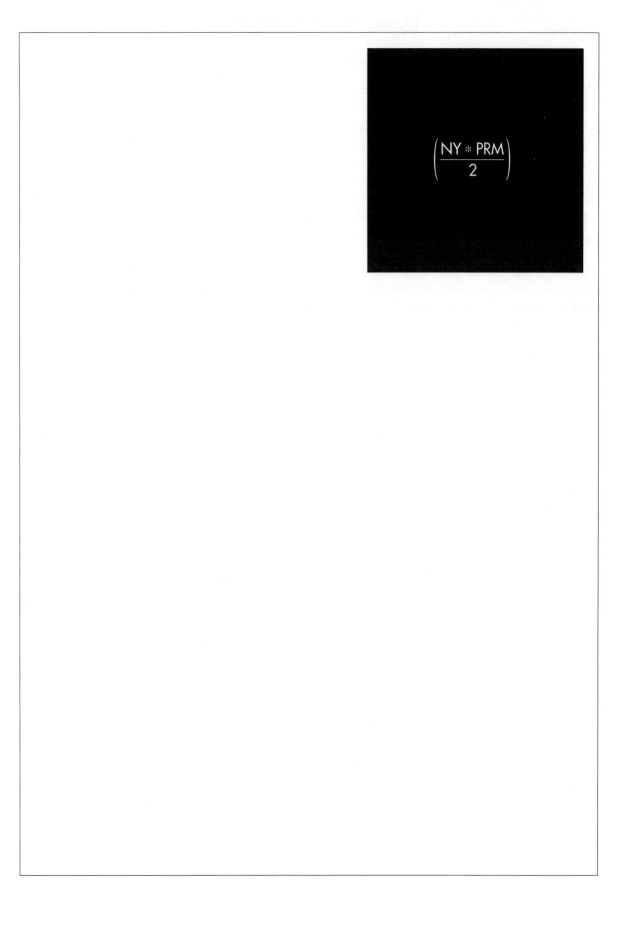

$$\left( \frac{NY * PRM}{2} \right)$$

# ESTIMATED YIELD FORMULA

[First guess for Yield (given Price) with more than one coupon period to redemption]

NOTE: There is no formula for converting price directly into yield for securities with more than one coupon period to redemption. However, by manipulation of the price formula (using estimated yields) an answer can be determined. To accomplish this, an estimated yield is substituted into the correct price formula. The result of this newly calculated price is then compared to the known price. Based on this comparison, the estimated yield previously substituted into the price formula is adjusted up or down, as required, to produce a corresponding adjustment in the next price to be calculated. Incremental adjustments are made to the estimated yield until the desired price is matched exactly or within prescribed limits. For a more detailed explanation of why the process above is needed and various specific methods see the section "Iteration Theory and Solving for Yield."

Formulas which can be used to calculate a first guess of yield for a regular payment bond are shown below. In many cases substituting the interest rate for the yield will provide a satisfactory starting point for the first calculation in the series of calculations necessary.

**Premium Bonds:**

$$Y = \frac{R * NY * 100 - PRM}{(NY * 100) - \left(\dfrac{NY * PRM}{2}\right) + \dfrac{PRM}{4}}$$

**Discount Bonds:**

$$Y = \frac{R * NY * 100 + DST}{(NY * 100) - \left(\dfrac{NY * DST}{2}\right) - \dfrac{DST}{4}}$$

where:

| | | |
|---|---|---|
| DST | = | Discount per $100 par value |
| NY | = | Number of years to redemption (as a decimal) |
| PRM | = | Premium per $100 par value |
| R | = | Annual interest rate (as a decimal) |
| Y | = | Approximation of yield to redemption (as a decimal) |

# EXAMPLE                    ESTIMATED YIELD FORMULA

## MUNICIPAL BOND

The following example illustrates the calculation of an estimated yield for municipal bond given a dollar price reflecting a premium.

| | |
|---|---|
| Settlement Date | 02/07/85 |
| Maturity Date | 02/01/94 |
| Day Count Basis | 30/360 |

$$\text{Price} = 101.203$$
$$\text{NY} = 8.9833333 = (8 + (^{354}\!/_{360}))$$
$$\text{PRM} = 1.203$$
$$\text{R} = 4\tfrac{1}{2}\% \ (0.045)$$
$$\text{Y} = 0.04338536^*$$

# EXAMPLE                    ESTIMATED YIELD FORMULA

## MUNICIPAL BOND

The following example illustrates the calculation of an estimated yield for municipal bond given a dollar price reflecting a discount.

| | |
|---|---|
| Settlement Date | 02/07/85 |
| Maturity Date | 07/01/96 |
| Day Count Basis | 30/360 |

$$\text{Price} = 99.525$$
$$\text{DST} = 0.475$$
$$\text{NY} = 11.4833333 = (11 + (^{144}\!/_{360}))$$
$$\text{R} = 4\tfrac{1}{2}\% \ (0.045)$$
$$\text{Y} = 0.04552954^*$$

---

*This is only an approximation for yield, **not** the actual yield

# NATIONAL ASSOCIATION OF SECURITIES DEALERS

Uniform Practice Code Section 46

## Interest to be added to the dollar price

(a) In the settlement of contracts in interest-paying securities other than for "cash," there shall be added to the dollar price interest at the rate specified in the security, computed up to but not including the fifth business day following the date of the transaction. In transactions for "cash," interest shall be added to the dollar price at the rate specified in the security up to but not including the date of transaction.

## Basis of Interest

(b) Interest shall be computed on the basis of a 360-day year, i.e., every calendar month shall be considered to be ½ of 360 days; every period from a date in one month to the same date in the following month shall be considered to be 30 days.

*Note: the number of elapsed days should be computed in accordance with the examples given the following table:*

*From 1st to 30th of the same month to be figured as 29 days.*

*From 1st to 31st of the same month to be figured as 30 days.*

*From 1st to 1st of the following month to be figured as 30 days.*

*From 1st to 28th of February to be figured as 27 days.*

*From the 23rd of February to the 3rd of March is to be figured as 10 days.*

*From the 15th of May to the 6th of June is to be figured as 21 days.*

*Where interest is a payable on 30th or 31st of the month:*

*From 30th or 31st to 1st of the following month to be figured as 1 day.*

*From 30th or 31st to 30th of the following month to be figured as 30 days.*

*From 30th or 31st to 31st of the following month to be figured as 30 days.*

*From 30th or 31st to 1st of the second following month to be figured as 1 month, 1 day.*

# MUNICIPAL SECURITIES RULEMAKING BOARD RULE G-33

(a) *Accrued Interest.* Accrued interest shall be computed in accordance with the following formula:

$$\text{Interest} = \text{Rate} * \text{Par Value of Transaction} * \frac{\text{Number of Days}}{\text{Number of Days in Year}}$$

For purposes of this formula, the "number of days" shall be deemed to be the number of days from the previous interest payment date (from the dated date, in the case of first coupons) up to, but not including, the settlement date. The "number of days" and the "number of days in year" shall be counted in accordance with the requirements of section (e) below.

(b) *Interest-Bearing Securities*

(i) *Dollar Price.* For transactions in interest-bearing securities effected on the basis of yield the resulting dollar price shall be computed in accordance with the following provisions:

(A) *Securities Paying Interest Solely at Redemption.* Except as otherwise provided in this section (b), the dollar price for a transaction in a security paying interest solely at redemption shall be computed in accordance with the following formula:

$$P = \left[\frac{RV + \left(\frac{DIR}{B} * R\right)}{1 + \frac{DIR - A}{B} * Y}\right] - \left[\frac{A}{B} * R\right]$$

For purposes of this formula the symbols shall be defined as follows:

"A" is the number of accrued days from the beginning of the interest payment period to the settlement date (computed in accordance with the provisions of section (e) below);

"B" is the number of days in the year (computed in accordance with the provisions of section (e) below); "DIR" is the number of days from the issue date to the redemption date (computed in accordance with the provisions of section (e) below);

"P" is the dollar price of the security for each $100 par value (divided by 100);

"R" is the annual interest rate (expressed as a decimal):

"RV" is the redemption value of the security per $100 par value (divided by 100); and

"Y" is the yield price of the transaction (expressed as a decimal).

(B) *Securities with Periodic Interest Payments.*  Except as otherwise provided in this section (b), the dollar price for a transaction in a security with periodic interest payments shall be computed as follows:

(1) for securities with six months or less to redemption, the following formula shall be used:

$$P = \left[ \frac{\dfrac{RV}{100} + \dfrac{R}{M}}{1 + \left( \dfrac{E - A}{E} * \dfrac{Y}{M} \right)} \right] - \left[ \frac{A}{B} * R \right]$$

For purposes of this formula the symbols shall be defined as follows:

"A" is the number of accrued days from the beginning of the interest payment period to the settlement date (computed in accordance with the provisions of section (e) below);

"B" is the number of days in the year (computed in accordance with the provisions of section (e) below);

"E" is the number of days in the interest payment period in which the settlement date falls (computed in accordance with the provisions of section (e) below);

"M" is the number of interest payment periods per year standard for the security involved in the transaction;

"P" is the dollar price of the security for each $100 par value (divided by 100);

"R" is the annual interest rate (expressed as a decimal);

"RV" is the redemption value of the security per $100 par value; and

"Y" is the yield price of the transaction (expressed as a decimal).

(2) for securities with more than six months to redemption, the following formula shall be used:

$$P = \left[ \frac{RV}{\left(1 + \frac{Y}{2}\right)^{N-1+\frac{E-A}{E}}_{exp}} \right] + \left[ \sum_{K=1}^{N} \frac{100 * \frac{R}{2}}{\left(1 + \frac{Y}{2}\right)^{K-1+\frac{E-A}{E}}_{exp}} \right] - \left[ 100 * \frac{A}{B} * R \right]$$

For purposes of this formula the symbols shall be defined as follows:

"A" is the number of accrued days from the beginning of the interest payment period to the settlement date (computed in accordance with the provisions of section (e) below);

"B" is the number of days in the year (computed in accordance with the provisions of section (e) below);

"E" is the number of days in the interest payment period in which the settlement date falls (computed in accordance with the provisions of section (e) below);

"N" is the number of interest payments (expressed as a whole number) occurring between the settlement date and redemption date, including the payment on the redemption date;

"P" is the dollar price of the security for each $100 par value (divided by 100);

"R" is the annual interest rate (expressed as a decimal):

"RV" is the redemption value of the security per $100 par value; and

"Y" is the yield price of the transaction (expressed as a decimal).

For purposes of this formula the symbol "exp" shall signify that the preceding value shall be raised to the power indicated by the succeeding value; for purposes of this formula the symbol "K" shall signify successively each whole number from "1" to "N" inclusive; for purposes of this formula the symbol "sigma" shall signify that the succeeding term shall be computed for each value "K" and that the results of such computations shall be summed.

(ii) *Yield.* Yields on interest-bearing securities shall be computed in accordance with the following provisions:

(A) *Securities Paying Interest Solely at Redemption.* The yield of a transaction in a security paying interest solely at redemption shall be computed in accordance with the following formula:

$$Y = \left[ \frac{\left(1 + \left(\frac{DIR}{B} * R\right)\right) - \left(P + \left(\frac{A}{B} * R\right)\right)}{P + \left(\frac{A}{B} * R\right)} \right] * \frac{B}{DIR - A}$$

For purposes of this formula the symbols shall be defined as follows:

"A" is the number of accrued days from the beginning of the interest payment period to the settlement date (computed in accordance with the provisions of section (e) below);

"B" is the number of days in the year (computed in accordance with the provisions of section (e) below);

"DIR" is the number of days from the issue date to the redemption date (computed in accordance with the provisions of section (e) below);

"P" is the dollar price of the security for each $100 par value (divided by 100);

"R" is the annual interest rate (expressed as a decimal):

"RV" is the redemption value of the security per $100 par value (divided by 100); and

"Y" is the yield on the investment if the security is held to redemption (expressed as a decimal).

(B) Securities with Periodic Interest Payments. The yield of a transaction in a security with periodic interest payment shall be computed at follows:

(1) for securities with six months or less to redemption, the following formula shall be used:

$$Y = \left[ \frac{\left( \frac{RV}{100} + \frac{R}{M} \right) - \left( P + \left( \frac{A}{E} * \frac{R}{M} \right) \right)}{P + \left( \frac{A}{E} * \frac{R}{M} \right)} \right] * \left[ \frac{M * E}{E - A} \right]$$

For purposes of this formula the symbols shall be defined as follows:

"A" is the number of accrued days from the beginning of the interest payment period to the settlement date (computed in accordance with the provisions of section (e) below);

"E" is the number of days in the interest payment period in which the settlement date falls (computed in accordance with the provisions of section (e) below);

"M" is the number of interest payment periods per year standard for the security involved in the transaction;

"P" is the dollar price of the security for each $100 par value (divided by 100);

"R" is the annual interest rate (expressed as a decimal):

"RV" is the redemption value of the security per $100 par value; and

"Y" is the yield on the investment if the security is held to redemption (expressed as a decimal).

(2) for securities with more than six months to redemption the formula set forth in item (2) of subparagraph (b)(i)(B) shall be used.

(c) *Discounted Securities.*

(i) *Dollar Price.* For transaction in discounted securities, the dollar price shall be computed in accordance with the following provisions:

(A) The dollar price of a discounted security, other than a discounted security traded with a yield-equivalent basis, shall be computed in accordance with the following formula:

$$P = [RV] - \left[ DR * RV * \frac{DSM}{B} \right]$$

For purposes of this formula the symbols shall be defined as follows:

"B" is the number of days in the year (computed in accordance with the provisions of section (e) below);

"DR" is the discount rate (expressed as a decimal);

"DSM" is the number of days from the settlement date of the transaction to the maturity date (computed in accordance with the provisions of section (e) below);

"P" is the dollar price of the security for each $100 par value; and

"RV" is the redemption value of the security per $100 par value.

(B) The dollar price of a discounted security traded on a yield-equivalent basis shall be computed in accordance with the formula set forth in subparagraph (b)(i)(A).

(ii) *Return on Investment.* The return on investment for a discounted security shall be computed in accordance with the following provisions:

(A) The return on investment for a discounted security, other than a discounted security traded on a yield-equivalent basis, shall be computed in accordance with the following formula:

$$IR = \left[\frac{RV - P}{P}\right] * \left[\frac{B}{DSM}\right]$$

For purposes of this formula the symbols shall be defined as follows:

"B" is the number of days in the year (computed in accordance with the provisions of section (e) below);

"DSM" is the number of days from the settlement date of the transaction to the maturity date (computed in accordance with the provisions of section (e) below);

"IR" is the annual return on investment if the security is held to maturity (expressed as a decimal);

"P" is the dollar price of the security for each $100 par value; and

"RV" is the redemption value of the security per $100 par value.

(B) The yield of a discounted security traded on a yield-equivalent basis shall be computed in accordance with the formula set forth in subparagraph (b)(ii)(A).

(d) *Standard of Accuracy; Truncation.*

(i) *Intermediate Values.* All values used in computations of accrued interest, yield, and dollar price shall be computed to not less than ten decimal places.

(ii) *Results of Computations.* Results of computation shall be presented in accordance with the following:

(A) Accrued interest shall be truncated to three decimal place and rounded to two decimal places immediately prior to presentation of total accrued interest amount on the confirmation;

(B) Dollar prices shall be truncated to three decimal places immediately prior to presentation of dollar price on the confirmation and computation of extended principal; and

(C)  Yields shall be truncated to four decimal places, and rounded to three decimal places, provided, however, that for purposes of confirmation display as required under rule G-15 (a)(viii)(B) yields accurate to the nearest .05 percentage points shall be deemed satisfactory.

Numbers shall be rounded, where required, in the following manner: if the last digit after truncation is five or above, the preceding digit shall be increased to the next highest number, and the last digit shall be discarded.

(e)  *Day Counting.*

(i)  *Day Count Basis.*  Computations under the requirements of this rule shall be made on the basis of a thirty-day month and a three-hundred-sixty-day year, or, in the face of computations on securities paying interest solely at redemption, on the day count basis selected by the issuer of the securities.

(ii)  *Day Count Formula.*  For purposes of this rule, computation of day counts on the basis of a thirty-date month and a three-hundred-sixty-day year shall be made in accordance with the following formula.

$$\text{Number of Days} = (Y2 - Y1) * 360 + (M2 - M1) * 30 + (D2 - D1)$$

For purposes of this formula the symbols shall be defined as follows:
"M1" is the month of the date on which the computation period begins;

"D1" is the day of the date on which the computation period begins;

"Y1" is the year of the date on which the computation period begins;

"M2" is the month of the date on which the computation period ends;

"D2" is the day of the date on which the computation period ends; and

"Y2" is the year of the date on which the computation period ends.

For purposes of this formula, if the symbol "D2" has a value of "31," and the symbol "D1" has a value of "30" or "31," the value of the symbol "D2" shall be changed to "30." If the symbol "D1" has value of "31," the value of the symbol "D1" shall be changed to "30." For purposes of this rule time periods be computed to include the day specified in the rule for the beginning of the period but not to include the day specified for the end of the period.

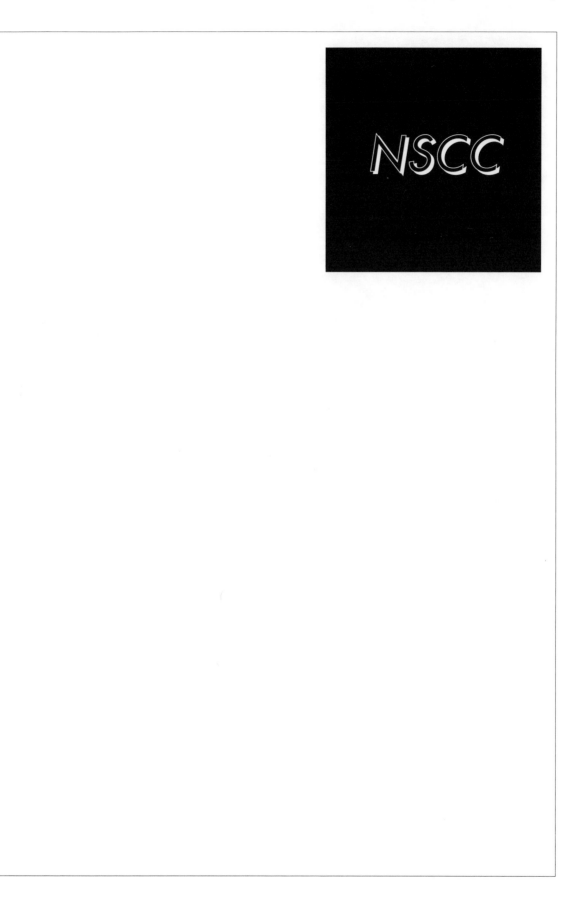

Exact Match/Price Submission (Column 49-59)

When-issued trades are matched on an exact one-for-one basis without allowing for a seller value difference ($.05 per $1,000.00) as is done in the secondary market.

Trades submitted with a dollar price (Column 60 = 0) only compare with like dollar price submission; trades submitted on a yield or yield plus/minus concession basis (Column 60 = 2) only compare with like submission. Concessions must be submitted per $100. Both sides must submit the identical information in the same price code format for the trade to compare. Equivalent yields and dollar prices will not compare.

NSCC recommends that dollar price transactions be submitted on separate trade blotters from yield or yield plus/minus concession basis transactions. Secondary market transactions with contract amounts should also be submitted separately. This helps reduce processing errors which result in rejected and uncompared trades.

The purpose of this section is to provide the user of this book with a common base for comparison of the calculation formulas.  The user may process these benchmark problems through his current system (whether it be manual or automated) and compare his results with those presented here.

The benchmarks were selected because they test areas of the calculations which are known to cause discrepancies in the industry due to incorrect implementation of the formulas.  The values of the variables and the results of the calculations were produced and verified using TIPS, Inc. (Trading & Investment • Programs & Systems, Inc.) software.

It is not our intention to imply here that favorable comparisons in these few calculations will guarantee that the user possesses a set of correct formulas - this can only be ascertained once the user's formulas and those presented herein are proven to be mathematically equivalent.


NOTE:  All occurances of accrued interest in the benchmarks are per $100.00 of par value.

# BENCHMARKS

## Benchmark # 1a

Treasury Bond

| | |
|---|---|
| Settlement date | 03/01/93 |
| Maturity date | 03/01/07 |
| Issue/dated date | 03/01/83 |
| First coupon date | 09/01/83 |
| Day count basis | Actual/Actual |

**Definition of Variables (Formula 7)**

| | | | |
|---|---|---|---|
| A | = | 0 | (03/01/93 - 03/01/93) |
| DSC | = | 184 | (03/01/93 - 09/01/93) |
| E | = | 184 | (03/01/93 - 09/01/93) |
| M | = | 2 | (semi-annual) |
| N | = | 28 | (03/01/93 - 03/01/07) |
| R | = | 0.100000 | (10.0000%) |
| RV | = | 100.0000 | |
| Y | = | 0.100000 | (10.0000%) |

**Result:**

| | | |
|---|---|---|
| Price | = | 100.000000 |
| Accrued interest | = | 0.00 |

## Benchmark # 1b

Agency Bond

| | |
|---|---|
| Settlement date | 03/01/93 |
| Maturity date | 03/01/07 |
| Issue/dated date | 03/01/83 |
| First coupon date | 09/01/83 |
| Day count basis | 30/360 |

**Definition of Variables (Formula 7)**

| | | | |
|---|---|---|---|
| A | = | 0 | (03/01/93 - 03/01/93) |
| DSC | = | 180 | (03/01/93 - 09/01/93) |
| E | = | 180 | (03/01/93 - 09/01/93) |
| M | = | 2 | (semi-annual) |
| N | = | 28 | (03/01/93 - 03/01/07) |
| R | = | 0.100000 | (10.0000%) |
| RV | = | 100.0000 | |
| Y | = | 0.100000 | (10.0000%) |

**Result:**

| | | |
|---|---|---|
| Price | = | 100.000000 |
| Accrued interest | = | 0.00 |

## Benchmark # 1c

Municipal Bond

| | |
|---|---|
| Settlement date | 03/01/93 |
| Maturity date | 03/01/07 |
| Issue/dated date | 03/01/83 |
| First coupon date | 09/01/83 |
| Day count basis | 30/360 |

**Definition of Variables (Formula 7)**

| | | | |
|---|---|---|---|
| A | = | 0 | (03/01/93 - 03/01/93) |
| DSC | = | 180 | (03/01/93 - 09/01/93) |
| E | = | 180 | (03/01/93 - 09/01/93) |
| M | = | 2 | (semi-annual) |
| N | = | 28 | (03/01/93 - 03/01/07) |
| R | = | 0.100000 | (10.0000%) |
| RV | = | 100.0000 | |
| Y | = | 0.100000 | (10.0000%) |

**Result:**

| | | |
|---|---|---|
| Price | = | 100.000 |
| Accrued interest | = | 0.00 |

## Benchmark # 1d

Corporate Bond

| | |
|---|---|
| Settlement date | 03/01/93 |
| Maturity date | 03/01/07 |
| Issue/dated date | 03/01/83 |
| First coupon date | 09/01/83 |
| Day count basis | 30/360 |

**Definition of Variables (Formula 7)**

| | | | |
|---|---|---|---|
| A | = | 0 | (03/01/93 - 03/01/93) |
| DSC | = | 180 | (03/01/93 - 09/01/93) |
| E | = | 180 | (03/01/93 - 09/01/93) |
| M | = | 2 | (semi-annual) |
| N | = | 28 | (03/01/93 - 03/01/07) |
| R | = | 0.100000 | (10.0000%) |
| RV | = | 100.0000 | |
| Y | = | 0.100000 | (10.0000%) |

**Result:**

| | | |
|---|---|---|
| Price | = | 100.000 |
| Accrued interest | = | 0.00 |

## BENCHMARK # 2A

Treasury Bond
Settlement date          03/01/93
Maturity date            01/01/07
Issue/dated date         01/01/83
First coupon date        07/01/83
Day count basis          Actual/Actual

### Definition of Variables (Formula 7)
| | | | |
|---|---|---|---|
| A | = | 59 | (01/01/93 - 03/01/93) |
| DSC | = | 122 | (03/01/93 - 07/01/93) |
| E | = | 181 | (01/01/93 - 07/01/93) |
| M | = | 2 | (semi-annual) |
| N | = | 28 | (03/01/93 - 01/01/07) |
| R | = | 0.100000 | (10.0000%) |
| RV | = | 100.0000 | |
| Y | = | 0.100000 | (10.0000%) |

### Result:
Price           =    99.973277
Accrued interest  =    1.63

## BENCHMARK # 2B

Agency Bond
Settlement date          03/01/93
Maturity date            01/01/07
Issue/dated date         01/01/83
First coupon date        07/01/83
Day count basis          30/360

### Definition of Variables (Formula 7)
| | | | |
|---|---|---|---|
| A | = | 60 | (01/01/93 - 03/01/93) |
| DSC | = | 120 | (03/01/93 - 07/01/93) |
| E | = | 180 | (01/01/93 - 07/01/93) |
| M | = | 2 | (semi-annual) |
| N | = | 28 | (03/01/93 - 01/01/07) |
| R | = | 0.100000 | (10.0000%) |
| RV | = | 100.0000 | |
| Y | = | 0.100000 | (10.0000%) |

### Result:
Price           =    99.972969
Accrued interest  =    1.67

## BENCHMARK # 2C

Municipal Bond
Settlement date          03/01/93
Maturity date            01/01/07
Issue/dated date         01/01/83
First coupon date        07/01/83
Day count basis          30/360

### Definition of Variables (Formula 7)
| | | | |
|---|---|---|---|
| A | = | 60 | (01/01/93 - 03/01/93) |
| DSC | = | 120 | (03/01/93 - 07/01/93) |
| E | = | 180 | (01/01/93 - 07/01/93) |
| M | = | 2 | (semi-annual) |
| N | = | 28 | (03/01/93 - 01/01/07) |
| R | = | 0.100000 | (10.0000%) |
| RV | = | 100.0000 | |
| Y | = | 0.100000 | (10.0000%) |

### Result:
Price           =    99.972
Accrued interest  =    1.67

## BENCHMARK # 2D

Corporate Bond
Settlement date          03/01/93
Maturity date            01/01/07
Issue/dated date         01/01/83
First coupon date        07/01/83
Day count basis          30/360

### Definition of Variables (Formula 7)
| | | | |
|---|---|---|---|
| A | = | 60 | (01/01/93 - 03/01/93) |
| DSC | = | 120 | (03/01/93 - 07/01/93) |
| E | = | 180 | (01/01/93 - 07/01/93) |
| M | = | 2 | (semi-annual) |
| N | = | 28 | (03/01/93 - 01/01/07) |
| R | = | 0.100000 | (10.0000%) |
| RV | = | 100.0000 | |
| Y | = | 0.100000 | (10.0000%) |

### Result:
Price           =    99.972
Accrued interest  =    1.67

## BENCHMARK # 3A

Treasury Bond

| | |
|---|---|
| Settlement date | 02/28/93 |
| Maturity date | 01/01/07 |
| Issue/dated date | 01/01/83 |
| First coupon date | 07/01/83 |
| Day count basis | Actual/Actual |

### Definition of Variables (Formula 7)

| | | | |
|---|---|---|---|
| A | = | 58 | (01/01/93 - 02/28/93) |
| DSC | = | 123 | (02/28/93 - 07/01/93) |
| E | = | 181 | (01/01/93 - 07/01/93) |
| M | = | 2 | (semi-annual) |
| N | = | 28 | (02/28/93 - 01/01/07) |
| R | = | 0.100000 | (10.0000%) |
| RV | = | 100.0000 | |
| Y | = | 0.100000 | (10.0000%) |

**Result:**

| | | |
|---|---|---|
| Price | = | 99.973517 |
| Accrued interest | = | 1.60 |

## BENCHMARK # 3B

Agency Bond

| | |
|---|---|
| Settlement date | 02/28/93 |
| Maturity date | 01/01/07 |
| Issue/dated date | 01/01/83 |
| First coupon date | 07/01/83 |
| Day count basis | 30/360 |

### Definition of Variables (Formula 7)

| | | | |
|---|---|---|---|
| A | = | 57 | (01/01/93 - 02/28/93) |
| DSC | = | 123 | (02/28/93 - 07/01/93) |
| E | = | 180 | (01/01/93 - 07/01/93) |
| M | = | 2 | (semi-annual) |
| N | = | 28 | (02/28/93 - 01/01/07) |
| R | = | 0.100000 | (10.0000%) |
| RV | = | 100.0000 | |
| Y | = | 0.100000 | (10.0000%) |

**Result:**

| | | |
|---|---|---|
| Price | = | 99.973686 |
| Accrued interest | = | 1.58 |

## BENCHMARK # 3C

Municipal Bond

| | |
|---|---|
| Settlement date | 02/28/93 |
| Maturity date | 01/01/07 |
| Issue/dated date | 01/01/83 |
| First coupon date | 07/01/83 |
| Day count basis | 30/360 |

### Definition of Variables (Formula 7)

| | | | |
|---|---|---|---|
| A | = | 57 | (01/01/93 - 02/28/93) |
| DSC | = | 123 | (02/28/93 - 07/01/93) |
| E | = | 180 | (01/01/93 - 07/01/93) |
| M | = | 2 | (semi-annual) |
| N | = | 28 | (02/28/93 - 01/01/07) |
| R | = | 0.100000 | (10.0000%) |
| RV | = | 100.0000 | |
| Y | = | 0.100000 | (10.0000%) |

**Result:**

| | | |
|---|---|---|
| Price | = | 99.973 |
| Accrued interest | = | 1.58 |

## BENCHMARK # 3D

Corporate Bond

| | |
|---|---|
| Settlement date | 02/28/93 |
| Maturity date | 01/01/07 |
| Issue/dated date | 01/01/83 |
| First coupon date | 07/01/83 |
| Day count basis | 30/360 |

### Definition of Variables (Formula 7)

| | | | |
|---|---|---|---|
| A | = | 57 | (01/01/93 - 02/28/93) |
| DSC | = | 123 | (02/28/93 - 07/01/93) |
| E | = | 180 | (01/01/93 - 07/01/93) |
| M | = | 2 | (semi-annual) |
| N | = | 28 | (02/28/93 - 01/01/07) |
| R | = | 0.100000 | (10.0000%) |
| RV | = | 100.0000 | |
| Y | = | 0.100000 | (10.0000%) |

**Result:**

| | | |
|---|---|---|
| Price | = | 99.973 |
| Accrued interest | = | 1.58 |

## BENCHMARK # 4A

Treasury Bond
| | |
|---|---|
| Settlement date | 01/30/93 |
| Maturity date | 01/31/07 |
| Issue/dated date | 01/31/83 |
| First coupon date | 07/31/83 |
| Day count basis | Actual/Actual |

**Definition of Variables (Formula 7)**

| | | | |
|---|---|---|---|
| A | = | 183 | (07/31/92 - 01/30/93) |
| DSC | = | 1 | (01/30/93 - 01/31/93) |
| E | = | 184 | (07/31/92 - 01/31/93) |
| M | = | 2 | (semi-annual) |
| N | = | 29 | (01/30/93 - 01/31/07) |
| R | = | 0.100000 | (10.0000%) |
| RV | = | 100.0000 | |
| Y | = | 0.100000 | (10.0000%) |

**Result:**
| | | |
|---|---|---|
| Price | = | 99.999335 |
| Accrued interest | = | 4.97 |

## BENCHMARK # 4B

Agency Bond
| | |
|---|---|
| Settlement date | 01/30/93 |
| Maturity date | 01/31/07 |
| Issue/dated date | 01/31/83 |
| First coupon date | 07/31/83 |
| Day count basis | 30/360 |

**Definition of Variables (Formula 7)**

| | | | |
|---|---|---|---|
| A | = | 180 | (07/31/92 - 01/30/93) |
| DSC | = | 0 | (01/30/93 - 01/31/93) |
| E | = | 180 | (07/31/92 - 01/31/93) |
| M | = | 2 | (semi-annual) |
| N | = | 29 | (01/30/93 - 01/31/07) |
| R | = | 0.100000 | (10.0000%) |
| RV | = | 100.0000 | |
| Y | = | 0.100000 | (10.0000%) |

**Result:**
| | | |
|---|---|---|
| Price | = | 100.000000 |
| Accrued interest | = | 5.00 |

## BENCHMARK # 4C

Municipal Bond
| | |
|---|---|
| Settlement date | 01/30/93 |
| Maturity date | 01/31/07 |
| Issue/dated date | 01/31/83 |
| First coupon date | 07/31/83 |
| Day count basis | 30/360 |

**Definition of Variables (Formula 7)**

| | | | |
|---|---|---|---|
| A | = | 180 | (07/31/92 - 01/30/93) |
| DSC | = | 0 | (01/30/93 - 01/31/93) |
| E | = | 180 | (07/31/92 - 01/31/93) |
| M | = | 2 | (semi-annual) |
| N | = | 29 | (01/30/93 - 01/31/07) |
| R | = | 0.100000 | (10.0000%) |
| RV | = | 100.0000 | |
| Y | = | 0.100000 | (10.0000%) |

**Result:**
| | | |
|---|---|---|
| Price | = | 100.000 |
| Accrued interest | = | 5.00 |

## BENCHMARK # 4D

Corporate Bond
| | |
|---|---|
| Settlement date | 01/30/93 |
| Maturity date | 01/31/07 |
| Issue/dated date | 01/31/83 |
| First coupon date | 07/31/83 |
| Day count basis | 30/360 |

**Definition of Variables (Formula 7)**

| | | | |
|---|---|---|---|
| A | = | 180 | (07/31/92 - 01/30/93) |
| DSC | = | 0 | (01/30/93 - 01/31/93) |
| E | = | 180 | (07/31/92 - 01/31/93) |
| M | = | 2 | (semi-annual) |
| N | = | 29 | (01/30/93 - 01/31/07) |
| R | = | 0.100000 | (10.0000%) |
| RV | = | 100.0000 | |
| Y | = | 0.100000 | (10.0000%) |

**Result:**
| | | |
|---|---|---|
| Price | = | 100.000 |
| Accrued interest | = | 5.00 |

## BENCHMARK # 5A

Treasury Bond
| | |
|---|---|
| Settlement date | 03/01/93 |
| Maturity date | 01/31/07 |
| Issue/dated date | 01/31/83 |
| First coupon date | 07/31/83 |
| Day count basis | Actual/Actual |

**Definition of Variables (Formula 7)**

| | | | |
|---|---|---|---|
| A | = | 29 | (01/31/93 - 03/01/93) |
| DSC | = | 152 | (03/01/93 - 07/31/93) |
| E | = | 181 | (01/31/93 - 07/31/93) |
| M | = | 2 | (semi-annual) |
| N | = | 28 | (03/01/93 - 01/31/07) |
| R | = | 0.100000 | (10.0000%) |
| RV | = | 100.0000 | |
| Y | = | 0.100000 | (10.0000%) |

**Result:**

| | | |
|---|---|---|
| Price | = | 99.983679 |
| Accrued interest | = | 0.80 |

## BENCHMARK # 5B

Agency Bond
| | |
|---|---|
| Settlement date | 03/01/93 |
| Maturity date | 01/31/07 |
| Issue/dated date | 01/31/83 |
| First coupon date | 07/31/83 |
| Day count basis | 30/360 |

**Definition of Variables (Formula 7)**

| | | | |
|---|---|---|---|
| A | = | 31 | (01/31/93 - 03/01/93) |
| DSC | = | 149 | (03/01/93 - 07/31/93) |
| E | = | 180 | (01/31/93 - 07/31/93) |
| M | = | 2 | (semi-annual) |
| N | = | 28 | (03/01/93 - 01/31/07) |
| R | = | 0.100000 | (10.0000%) |
| RV | = | 100.0000 | |
| Y | = | 0.100000 | (10.0000%) |

**Result:**

| | | |
|---|---|---|
| Price | = | 99.982704 |
| Accrued interest | = | 0.86 |

## BENCHMARK # 5C

Municipal Bond
| | |
|---|---|
| Settlement date | 03/01/93 |
| Maturity date | 01/31/07 |
| Issue/dated date | 01/31/83 |
| First coupon date | 07/31/83 |
| Day count basis | 30/360 |

**Definition of Variables (Formula 7)**

| | | | |
|---|---|---|---|
| A | = | 31 | (01/31/93 - 03/01/93) |
| DSC | = | 149 | (03/01/93 - 07/31/93) |
| E | = | 180 | (01/31/93 - 07/31/93) |
| M | = | 2 | (semi-annual) |
| N | = | 28 | (03/01/93 - 01/31/07) |
| R | = | 0.100000 | (10.0000%) |
| RV | = | 100.0000 | |
| Y | = | 0.100000 | (10.0000%) |

**Result:**

| | | |
|---|---|---|
| Price | = | 99.982 |
| Accrued interest | = | 0.86 |

## BENCHMARK # 5D

Corporate Bond
| | |
|---|---|
| Settlement date | 03/01/93 |
| Maturity date | 01/31/07 |
| Issue/dated date | 01/31/83 |
| First coupon date | 07/31/83 |
| Day count basis | 30/360 |

**Definition of Variables (Formula 7)**

| | | | |
|---|---|---|---|
| A | = | 31 | (01/31/93 - 03/01/93) |
| DSC | = | 149 | (03/01/93 - 07/31/93) |
| E | = | 180 | (01/31/93 - 07/31/93) |
| M | = | 2 | (semi-annual) |
| N | = | 28 | (03/01/93 - 01/31/07) |
| R | = | 0.100000 | (10.0000%) |
| RV | = | 100.0000 | |
| Y | = | 0.100000 | (10.0000%) |

**Result:**

| | | |
|---|---|---|
| Price | = | 99.982 |
| Accrued interest | = | 0.86 |

## BENCHMARK # 6A

Treasury Bond

| | |
|---|---|
| Settlement date | 12/04/93 |
| Maturity date | 03/01/07 |
| Issue/dated date | 05/01/93 |
| First coupon date | 03/01/94 |
| Day count basis | Actual/Actual |

### Definition of Variables (Formula 9)

| | | | |
|---|---|---|---|
| A1 | = | 123 | (05/01/93 - 09/01/93) |
| A2 | = | 94 | (09/01/93 - 12/04/93) |
| DFC1 | = | 123 | (05/01/93 - 09/01/93) |
| DFC2 | = | 181 | (09/01/93 - 03/01/94) |
| DSC | = | 87 | (12/04/93 - 03/01/94) |
| E | = | 181 | (09/01/93 - 03/01/94) |
| M | = | 2 | (semi-annual) |
| N | = | 26 | (03/01/94 - 03/01/07) |
| NCF | = | 2 | (05/01/93 - 03/01/94) |
| $NLF_1$ | = | 184 | (03/01/93 - 09/01/93) |
| $NLF_2$ | = | 181 | (09/01/93 - 03/01/94) |
| $Nqf$ | = | 0 | (12/04/93 - 03/01/94) |
| R | = | 0.085000 | (8.5000%) |
| RV | = | 100.0000 | |
| Y | = | 0.100000 | (10.0000%) |

**Result:**

| | | |
|---|---|---|
| Price | = | 89.029089 |
| Accrued interest | = | 5.05 |

## BENCHMARK # 6B

Agency Bond

| | |
|---|---|
| Settlement date | 12/04/93 |
| Maturity date | 03/01/07 |
| Issue/dated date | 05/01/93 |
| First coupon date | 03/01/94 |
| Day count basis | 30/360 |

### Definition of Variables (Formula 9)

| | | | |
|---|---|---|---|
| A1 | = | 120 | (05/01/93 - 09/01/93) |
| A2 | = | 93 | (09/01/93 - 12/04/93) |
| DFC1 | = | 120 | (05/01/93 - 09/01/93) |
| DFC2 | = | 180 | (09/01/93 - 03/01/94) |
| DSC | = | 87 | (12/04/93 - 03/01/94) |
| E | = | 180 | (09/01/93 - 03/01/94) |
| M | = | 2 | (semi-annual) |
| N | = | 26 | (03/01/94 - 03/01/07) |
| NCF | = | 2 | (05/01/93 - 03/01/94) |
| $NLF_1$ | = | 180 | (03/01/93 - 09/01/93) |
| $NLF_2$ | = | 180 | (09/01/93 - 03/01/94) |
| $Nqf$ | = | 0 | (12/04/93 - 03/01/94) |
| R | = | 0.085000 | (8.5000%) |
| RV | = | 100.0000 | |
| Y | = | 0.100000 | (10.0000%) |

**Result:**

| | | |
|---|---|---|
| Price | = | 89.028361 |
| Accrued interest | = | 5.03 |

## BENCHMARK # 6C

Municipal Bond

| | |
|---|---|
| Settlement date | 12/04/93 |
| Maturity date | 03/01/07 |
| Issue/dated date | 05/01/93 |
| First coupon date | 03/01/94 |
| Day count basis | 30/360 |

### Definition of Variables (Formula 7)

| | | | |
|---|---|---|---|
| A | = | 93 | (09/01/93 - 12/04/93) |
| DSC | = | 87 | (12/04/93 - 03/01/94) |
| E | = | 180 | (09/01/93 - 03/01/94) |
| M | = | 2 | (semi-annual) |
| N | = | 27 | (12/04/93 - 03/01/07) |
| R | = | 0.085000 | (8.5000%) |
| RV | = | 100.0000 | |
| Y | = | 0.100000 | (10.0000%) |

**Result:**

| | | |
|---|---|---|
| Price | = | 89.094 |
| Accrued interest | = | 5.03 |

Note: These results are calculated useing M.S.R.B. Rule G–33 in which odd first and/or odd last periods are ignored in calculating price/yield. The accrued interest however, is based on the actual number of days accrued.

## BENCHMARK # 6D

Corporate Bond

| | |
|---|---|
| Settlement date | 12/04/93 |
| Maturity date | 03/01/07 |
| Issue/dated date | 05/01/93 |
| First coupon date | 03/01/94 |
| Day count basis | 30/360 |

### Definition of Variables (Formula 9)

| | | | |
|---|---|---|---|
| A1 | = | 120 | (05/01/93 - 09/01/93) |
| A2 | = | 93 | (09/01/93 - 12/04/93) |
| DFC1 | = | 120 | (05/01/93 - 09/01/93) |
| DFC2 | = | 180 | (09/01/93 - 03/01/94) |
| DSC | = | 87 | (12/04/93 - 03/01/94) |
| E | = | 180 | (09/01/93 - 03/01/94) |
| M | = | 2 | (semi-annual) |
| N | = | 26 | (03/01/94 - 03/01/07) |
| NCF | = | 2 | (05/01/93 - 03/01/94) |
| $NLF_1$ | = | 180 | (03/01/93 - 09/01/93) |
| $NLF_2$ | = | 180 | (09/01/93 - 03/01/94) |
| $Nqf$ | = | 0 | (12/04/93 - 03/01/94) |
| R | = | 0.085000 | (8.5000%) |
| RV | = | 100.0000 | |
| Y | = | 0.100000 | (10.0000%) |

**Result:**

| | | |
|---|---|---|
| Price | = | 89.028 |
| Accrued interest | = | 5.03 |

## Benchmark # 7A

Treasury Bond
| | |
|---|---|
| Settlement date | 05/31/93 |
| Maturity date | 03/01/07 |
| Issue/dated date | 05/01/93 |
| First coupon date | 03/01/94 |
| Day count basis | Actual/Actual |

**Definition of Variables (Formula 9)**

| | | | |
|---|---|---|---|
| $A1$ | = | 30 | (05/01/93 - 05/31/93) |
| $A2$ | = | 0 | |
| $DFC1$ | = | 123 | (05/01/93 - 09/01/93) |
| $DFC2$ | = | 181 | (09/01/93 - 03/01/94) |
| $DSC$ | = | 93 | (05/31/93 - 09/01/93) |
| $E$ | = | 184 | (03/01/93 - 09/01/93) |
| $M$ | = | 2 | (semi-annual) |
| $N$ | = | 26 | (03/01/94 - 03/01/07) |
| $NCF$ | = | 2 | (05/01/93 - 03/01/94) |
| $NLF_1$ | = | 184 | (03/01/93 - 09/01/93) |
| $NLF_2$ | = | 181 | (09/01/93 - 03/01/94) |
| $Nqf$ | = | 1 | (05/31/93 - 03/01/94) |
| $R$ | = | 0.085000 | (8.5000%) |
| $RV$ | = | 100.0000 | |
| $Y$ | = | 0.100000 | (10.0000%) |

**Result:**

| | | |
|---|---|---|
| Price | = | 88.796274 |
| Accrued interest | = | 0.69 |

## Benchmark # 7B

Agency Bond
| | |
|---|---|
| Settlement date | 05/31/93 |
| Maturity date | 03/01/07 |
| Issue/dated date | 05/01/93 |
| First coupon date | 03/01/94 |
| Day count basis | 30/360 |

**Definition of Variables (Formula 9)**

| | | | |
|---|---|---|---|
| $A1$ | = | 30 | (05/01/93 - 05/31/93) |
| $A2$ | = | 0 | |
| $DFC1$ | = | 120 | (05/01/93 - 09/01/93) |
| $DFC2$ | = | 180 | (09/01/93 - 03/01/94) |
| $DSC$ | = | 90 | (05/31/93 - 09/01/93) |
| $E$ | = | 180 | (03/01/93 - 09/01/93) |
| $M$ | = | 2 | (semi-annual) |
| $N$ | = | 26 | (03/01/94 - 03/01/07) |
| $NCF$ | = | 2 | (05/01/93 - 03/01/94) |
| $NLF_1$ | = | 180 | (03/01/93 - 09/01/93) |
| $NLF_2$ | = | 180 | (09/01/93 - 03/01/94) |
| $Nqf$ | = | 1 | (05/31/93 - 03/01/94) |
| $R$ | = | 0.085000 | (8.5000%) |
| $RV$ | = | 100.0000 | |
| $Y$ | = | 0.100000 | (10.0000%) |

**Result:**

| | | |
|---|---|---|
| Price | = | 88.797452 |
| Accrued interest | = | 0.71 |

## Benchmark # 7C

Municipal Bond
| | |
|---|---|
| Settlement date | 05/31/93 |
| Maturity date | 03/01/07 |
| Issue/dated date | 05/01/93 |
| First coupon date | 03/01/94 |
| Day count basis | 30/360 |

**Definition of Variables (Formula 7)**

| | | | |
|---|---|---|---|
| $A$ | = | 90 | (03/01/93 - 05/31/93) |
| $DSC$ | = | 90 | (05/31/93 - 09/01/93) |
| $E$ | = | 180 | (03/01/93 - 09/01/93) |
| $M$ | = | 2 | (semi-annual) |
| $N$ | = | 28 | (05/31/93 - 03/01/07) |
| $R$ | = | 0.085000 | (8.5000%) |
| $RV$ | = | 100.0000 | |
| $Y$ | = | 0.100000 | (10.0000%) |

**Result:**

| | | |
|---|---|---|
| Price | = | 88.894 |
| Accrued interest | = | 0.71 |

Note: These results are calculated useing M.S.R.B. Rule G–33 in which odd first and/or odd last periods are ignored in calculating price/yield. The accrued interest however, is based on the actual number of days accrued.

## Benchmark # 7D

Corporate Bond
| | |
|---|---|
| Settlement date | 05/31/93 |
| Maturity date | 03/01/07 |
| Issue/dated date | 05/01/93 |
| First coupon date | 03/01/94 |
| Day count basis | 30/360 |

**Definition of Variables (Formula 9)**

| | | | |
|---|---|---|---|
| $A1$ | = | 30 | (05/01/93 - 05/31/93) |
| $A2$ | = | 0 | |
| $DFC1$ | = | 120 | (05/01/93 - 09/01/93) |
| $DFC2$ | = | 180 | (09/01/93 - 03/01/94) |
| $DSC$ | = | 90 | (05/31/93 - 09/01/93) |
| $E$ | = | 180 | (03/01/93 - 09/01/93) |
| $M$ | = | 2 | (semi-annual) |
| $N$ | = | 26 | (03/01/94 - 03/01/07) |
| $NCF$ | = | 2 | (05/01/93 - 03/01/94) |
| $NLF_1$ | = | 180 | (03/01/93 - 09/01/93) |
| $NLF_2$ | = | 180 | (09/01/93 - 03/01/94) |
| $Nqf$ | = | 1 | (05/31/93 - 03/01/94) |
| $R$ | = | 0.085000 | (8.5000%) |
| $RV$ | = | 100.0000 | |
| $Y$ | = | 0.100000 | (10.0000%) |

**Result:**

| | | |
|---|---|---|
| Price | = | 88.797 |
| Accrued interest | = | 0.71 |

## BENCHMARK # 8A

Treasury Bond
Settlement date           12/02/93
Maturity date             03/01/07
Issue/dated date          10/01/93
First coupon date         03/01/94
Day count basis           Actual/Actual

### Definition of Variables (Formula 8)

| | | | |
|---|---|---|---|
| A | = | 62 | (10/01/93 - 12/02/93) |
| DFC | = | 151 | (10/01/93 - 03/01/94) |
| DSC | = | 89 | (12/02/93 - 03/01/94) |
| E | = | 181 | (09/01/93 - 03/01/94) |
| M | = | 2 | (semi-annual) |
| N | = | 27 | (12/02/93 - 03/01/07) |
| R | = | 0.055000 | (5.5000%) |
| RV | = | 100.0000 | |
| Y | = | 0.100000 | (10.0000%) |

### Result:

| | | |
|---|---|---|
| Price | = | 67.349860 |
| Accrued interest | = | 0.94 |

## BENCHMARK # 8B

Agency Bond
Settlement date           12/02/93
Maturity date             03/01/07
Issue/dated date          10/01/93
First coupon date         03/01/94
Day count basis           30/360

### Definition of Variables (Formula 8)

| | | | |
|---|---|---|---|
| A | = | 61 | (10/01/93 - 12/02/93) |
| DFC | = | 150 | (10/01/93 - 03/01/94) |
| DSC | = | 89 | (12/02/93 - 03/01/94) |
| E | = | 180 | (09/01/93 - 03/01/94) |
| M | = | 2 | (semi-annual) |
| N | = | 27 | (12/02/93 - 03/01/07) |
| R | = | 0.055000 | (5.5000%) |
| RV | = | 100.0000 | |
| Y | = | 0.100000 | (10.0000%) |

### Result:

| | | |
|---|---|---|
| Price | = | 67.348331 |
| Accrued interest | = | 0.93 |

## BENCHMARK # 8C

Municipal Bond
Settlement date           12/02/93
Maturity date             03/01/07
Issue/dated date          10/01/93
First coupon date         03/01/94
Day count basis           30/360

### Definition of Variables (Formula 7)

| | | | |
|---|---|---|---|
| A | = | 91 | (09/01/93 - 12/02/93) |
| DSC | = | 89 | (12/02/93 - 03/01/94) |
| E | = | 180 | (09/01/93 - 03/01/94) |
| M | = | 2 | (semi-annual) |
| N | = | 27 | (12/02/93 - 03/01/07) |
| R | = | 0.055000 | (5.5000%) |
| RV | = | 100.0000 | |
| Y | = | 0.100000 | (10.0000%) |

### Result:

| | | |
|---|---|---|
| Price | = | 67.337 |
| Accrued interest | = | 0.93 |

Note: These results are calculated useing M.S.R.B. Rule G–33 in which odd first and/or odd last periods are ignored in calculating price/yield. The accrued interest however, is based on the actual number of days accrued.

## BENCHMARK # 8D

Corporate Bond
Settlement date           12/02/93
Maturity date             03/01/07
Issue/dated date          10/01/93
First coupon date         03/01/94
Day count basis           30/360

### Definition of Variables (Formula 8)

| | | | |
|---|---|---|---|
| A | = | 61 | (10/01/93 - 12/02/93) |
| DFC | = | 150 | (10/01/93 - 03/01/94) |
| DSC | = | 89 | (12/02/93 - 03/01/94) |
| E | = | 180 | (09/01/93 - 03/01/94) |
| M | = | 2 | (semi-annual) |
| N | = | 27 | (12/02/93 - 03/01/07) |
| R | = | 0.055000 | (5.5000%) |
| RV | = | 100.0000 | |
| Y | = | 0.100000 | (10.0000%) |

### Result:

| | | |
|---|---|---|
| Price | = | 67.348 |
| Accrued interest | = | 0.93 |

## BENCHMARK # 9A

Treasury Bond
Settlement date ............ 03/01/93
Maturity date ............. 03/01/23
Issue/dated date .......... 01/01/93
First coupon date ......... 09/01/93
Day count basis ........... Actual/Actual

**Definition of Variables (Formula 9)**

| | | | |
|---|---|---|---|
| A1 | = | 59 | (01/01/93 - 03/01/93) |
| A2 | = | 0 | (03/01/93 - 03/01/93) |
| DFC1 | = | 59 | (01/01/93 - 03/01/93) |
| DFC2 | = | 184 | (03/01/93 - 09/01/93) |
| DSC | = | 184 | (03/01/93 - 09/01/93) |
| E | = | 184 | (03/01/93 - 09/01/93) |
| M | = | 2 | (semi-annual) |
| N | = | 59 | (09/01/93 - 03/01/23) |
| NCF | = | 2 | (01/01/93 - 09/01/93) |
| $NLF_1$ | = | 181 | (09/01/92 - 03/01/93) |
| $NLF_2$ | = | 184 | (03/01/93 - 09/01/93) |
| Nqf | = | 1 | (03/01/93 - 09/01/93) |
| R | = | 0.050000 | (5.0000%) |
| RV | = | 100.0000 | |
| Y | = | 0.060000 | (6.0000%) |

**Result:**
Price            =    86.138483
Accrued interest  =     0.81

## BENCHMARK # 9B

Agency Bond
Settlement date ............ 03/01/93
Maturity date ............. 03/01/23
Issue/dated date .......... 01/01/93
First coupon date ......... 09/01/93
Day count basis ........... 30/360

**Definition of Variables (Formula 9)**

| | | | |
|---|---|---|---|
| A1 | = | 60 | (01/01/93 - 03/01/93) |
| A2 | = | 0 | (03/01/93 - 03/01/93) |
| DFC1 | = | 60 | (01/01/93 - 03/01/93) |
| DFC2 | = | 180 | (03/01/93 - 09/01/93) |
| DSC | = | 180 | (03/01/93 - 09/01/93) |
| E | = | 180 | (03/01/93 - 09/01/93) |
| M | = | 2 | (semi-annual) |
| N | = | 59 | (09/01/93 - 03/01/23) |
| NCF | = | 2 | (01/01/93 - 09/01/93) |
| $NLF_1$ | = | 180 | (09/01/92 - 03/01/93) |
| $NLF_2$ | = | 180 | (03/01/93 - 09/01/93) |
| Nqf | = | 1 | (03/01/93 - 09/01/93) |
| R | = | 0.050000 | (5.0000%) |
| RV | = | 100.0000 | |
| Y | = | 0.060000 | (6.0000%) |

**Result:**
Price            =    86.137946
Accrued interest  =     0.83

## BENCHMARK # 9C

Municipal Bond
Settlement date ............ 03/01/93
Maturity date ............. 03/01/23
Issue/dated date .......... 01/01/93
First coupon date ......... 09/01/93
Day count basis ........... 30/360

**Definition of Variables (Formula 7)**

| | | | |
|---|---|---|---|
| A | = | 0 | (03/01/93 - 03/01/93) |
| DSC | = | 180 | (03/01/93 - 09/01/93) |
| E | = | 180 | (03/01/93 - 09/01/93) |
| M | = | 2 | (semi-annual) |
| N | = | 60 | (03/01/93 - 03/01/23) |
| R | = | 0.050000 | (5.0000%) |
| RV | = | 100.0000 | |
| Y | = | 0.060000 | (6.0000%) |

**Result:**
Price            =    86.162
Accrued interest  =     0.83

Note: These results are calculated useing M.S.R.B. Rule
G–33 in which odd first and/or odd last periods
are ignored in calculating price/yield. The
accrued interest however, is based on the actual
number of days accrued.

## BENCHMARK # 9D

Corporate Bond
Settlement date ............ 03/01/93
Maturity date ............. 03/01/23
Issue/dated date .......... 01/01/93
First coupon date ......... 09/01/93
Day count basis ........... 30/360

**Definition of Variables (Formula 9)**

| | | | |
|---|---|---|---|
| A1 | = | 60 | (01/01/93 - 03/01/93) |
| A2 | = | 0 | (03/01/93 - 03/01/93) |
| DFC1 | = | 60 | (01/01/93 - 03/01/93) |
| DFC2 | = | 180 | (03/01/93 - 09/01/93) |
| DSC | = | 180 | (03/01/93 - 09/01/93) |
| E | = | 180 | (03/01/93 - 09/01/93) |
| M | = | 2 | (semi-annual) |
| N | = | 59 | (09/01/93 - 03/01/23) |
| NCF | = | 2 | (01/01/93 - 09/01/93) |
| $NLF_1$ | = | 180 | (09/01/92 - 03/01/93) |
| $NLF_2$ | = | 180 | (03/01/93 - 09/01/93) |
| Nqf | = | 1 | (03/01/93 - 09/01/93) |
| R | = | 0.050000 | (5.0000%) |
| RV | = | 100.0000 | |
| Y | = | 0.060000 | (6.0000%) |

**Result:**
Price            =    86.137
Accrued interest  =     0.83

## BENCHMARK # 10A

Treasury Bond

| | |
|---|---|
| Settlement date | 04/01/93 |
| Maturity date | 03/01/23 |
| Issue/dated date | 01/01/93 |
| First coupon date | 09/01/93 |
| Day count basis | Actual/Actual |

### Definition of Variables (Formula 9)

| | | | |
|---|---|---|---|
| A1 | = | 59 | (01/01/93 - 03/01/93) |
| A2 | = | 31 | (03/01/93 - 04/01/93) |
| DFC1 | = | 59 | (01/01/93 - 03/01/93) |
| DFC2 | = | 184 | (03/01/93 - 09/01/93) |
| DSC | = | 153 | (04/01/93 - 09/01/93) |
| E | = | 184 | (03/01/93 - 09/01/93) |
| M | = | 2 | (semi-annual) |
| N | = | 59 | (09/01/93 - 03/01/23) |
| NCF | = | 2 | (01/01/93 - 09/01/93) |
| $NLF_1$ | = | 181 | (09/01/92 - 03/01/93) |
| $NLF_2$ | = | 184 | (03/01/93 - 09/01/93) |
| Nqf | = | 0 | (04/01/93 - 09/01/93) |
| R | = | 0.050000 | (5.0000%) |
| RV | = | 100.0000 | |
| Y | = | 0.060000 | (6.0000%) |

### Result:

| | | |
|---|---|---|
| Price | = | 86.151396 |
| Accrued interest | = | 1.24 |

## BENCHMARK # 10B

Agency Bond

| | |
|---|---|
| Settlement date | 04/01/93 |
| Maturity date | 03/01/23 |
| Issue/dated date | 01/01/93 |
| First coupon date | 09/01/93 |
| Day count basis | 30/360 |

### Definition of Variables (Formula 9)

| | | | |
|---|---|---|---|
| A1 | = | 60 | (01/01/93 - 03/01/93) |
| A2 | = | 30 | (03/01/93 - 04/01/93) |
| DFC1 | = | 60 | (01/01/93 - 03/01/93) |
| DFC2 | = | 180 | (03/01/93 - 09/01/93) |
| DSC | = | 150 | (04/01/93 - 09/01/93) |
| E | = | 180 | (03/01/93 - 09/01/93) |
| M | = | 2 | (semi-annual) |
| N | = | 59 | (09/01/93 - 03/01/23) |
| NCF | = | 2 | (01/01/93 - 09/01/93) |
| $NLF_1$ | = | 180 | (09/01/92 - 03/01/93) |
| $NLF_2$ | = | 180 | (03/01/93 - 09/01/93) |
| Nqf | = | 0 | (04/01/93 - 09/01/93) |
| R | = | 0.050000 | (5.0000%) |
| RV | = | 100.0000 | |
| Y | = | 0.060000 | (6.0000%) |

### Result:

| | | |
|---|---|---|
| Price | = | 86.150798 |
| Accrued interest | = | 1.25 |

## BENCHMARK # 10C

Municipal Bond

| | |
|---|---|
| Settlement date | 04/01/93 |
| Maturity date | 03/01/23 |
| Issue/dated date | 01/01/93 |
| First coupon date | 09/01/93 |
| Day count basis | 30/360 |

### Definition of Variables (Formula 7)

| | | | |
|---|---|---|---|
| A | = | 30 | (03/01/93 - 04/01/93) |
| DSC | = | 150 | (04/01/93 - 09/01/93) |
| E | = | 180 | (03/01/93 - 09/01/93) |
| M | = | 2 | (semi-annual) |
| N | = | 60 | (04/01/93 - 03/01/23) |
| R | = | 0.050000 | (5.0000%) |
| RV | = | 100.0000 | |
| Y | = | 0.060000 | (6.0000%) |

### Result:

| | | |
|---|---|---|
| Price | = | 86.171 |
| Accrued interest | = | 1.25 |

Note: These results are calculated useing M.S.R.B. Rule G–33 in which odd first and/or odd last periods are ignored in calculating price/yield. The accrued interest however, is based on the actual number of days accrued.

## BENCHMARK # 10D

Corporate Bond

| | |
|---|---|
| Settlement date | 04/01/93 |
| Maturity date | 03/01/23 |
| Issue/dated date | 01/01/93 |
| First coupon date | 09/01/93 |
| Day count basis | 30/360 |

### Definition of Variables (Formula 9)

| | | | |
|---|---|---|---|
| A1 | = | 60 | (01/01/93 - 03/01/93) |
| A2 | = | 30 | (03/01/93 - 04/01/93) |
| DFC1 | = | 60 | (01/01/93 - 03/01/93) |
| DFC2 | = | 180 | (03/01/93 - 09/01/93) |
| DSC | = | 150 | (04/01/93 - 09/01/93) |
| E | = | 180 | (03/01/93 - 09/01/93) |
| M | = | 2 | (semi-annual) |
| N | = | 59 | (09/01/93 - 03/01/23) |
| NCF | = | 2 | (01/01/93 - 09/01/93) |
| $NLF_1$ | = | 180 | (09/01/92 - 03/01/93) |
| $NLF_2$ | = | 180 | (03/01/93 - 09/01/93) |
| Nqf | = | 0 | (04/01/93 - 09/01/93) |
| R | = | 0.050000 | (5.0000%) |
| RV | = | 100.0000 | |
| Y | = | 0.060000 | (6.0000%) |

### Result:

| | | |
|---|---|---|
| Price | = | 86.150 |
| Accrued interest | = | 1.25 |

## BENCHMARK # 11A

Treasury Bond
| | | |
|---|---|---|
| Settlement date | 07/01/93 |
| Maturity date | 03/01/23 |
| Issue/dated date | 01/01/93 |
| First coupon date | 09/01/93 |
| Day count basis | Actual/Actual |

### Definition of Variables (Formula 9)

| | | | |
|---|---|---|---|
| A1 | = | 59 | (01/01/93 - 03/01/93) |
| A2 | = | 122 | (03/01/93 - 07/01/93) |
| DFC1 | = | 59 | (01/01/93 - 03/01/93) |
| DFC2 | = | 184 | (03/01/93 - 09/01/93) |
| DSC | = | 62 | (07/01/93 - 09/01/93) |
| E | = | 184 | (03/01/93 - 09/01/93) |
| M | = | 2 | (semi-annual) |
| N | = | 59 | (09/01/93 - 03/01/23) |
| NCF | = | 2 | (01/01/93 - 09/01/93) |
| $NLF_1$ | = | 181 | (09/01/92 - 03/01/93) |
| $NLF_2$ | = | 184 | (03/01/93 - 09/01/93) |
| Nqf | = | 0 | (07/01/93 - 09/01/93) |
| R | = | 0.050000 | (5.0000%) |
| RV | = | 100.0000 | |
| Y | = | 0.060000 | (6.0000%) |

### Result:
| | | |
|---|---|---|
| Price | = | 86.201863 |
| Accrued interest | = | 2.47 |

## BENCHMARK # 11B

Agency Bond
| | | |
|---|---|---|
| Settlement date | 07/01/93 |
| Maturity date | 03/01/23 |
| Issue/dated date | 01/01/93 |
| First coupon date | 09/01/93 |
| Day count basis | 30/360 |

### Definition of Variables (Formula 9)

| | | | |
|---|---|---|---|
| A1 | = | 60 | (01/01/93 - 03/01/93) |
| A2 | = | 120 | (03/01/93 - 07/01/93) |
| DFC1 | = | 60 | (01/01/93 - 03/01/93) |
| DFC2 | = | 180 | (03/01/93 - 09/01/93) |
| DSC | = | 60 | (07/01/93 - 09/01/93) |
| E | = | 180 | (03/01/93 - 09/01/93) |
| M | = | 2 | (semi-annual) |
| N | = | 59 | (09/01/93 - 03/01/23) |
| NCF | = | 2 | (01/01/93 - 09/01/93) |
| $NLF_1$ | = | 180 | (09/01/92 - 03/01/93) |
| $NLF_2$ | = | 180 | (03/01/93 - 09/01/93) |
| Nqf | = | 0 | (07/01/93 - 09/01/93) |
| R | = | 0.050000 | (5.0000%) |
| RV | = | 100.0000 | |
| Y | = | 0.060000 | (6.0000%) |

### Result:
| | | |
|---|---|---|
| Price | = | 86.202122 |
| Accrued interest | = | 2.50 |

## BENCHMARK # 11C

Municipal Bond
| | | |
|---|---|---|
| Settlement date | 07/01/93 |
| Maturity date | 03/01/23 |
| Issue/dated date | 01/01/93 |
| First coupon date | 09/01/93 |
| Day count basis | 30/360 |

### Definition of Variables (Formula 7)

| | | | |
|---|---|---|---|
| A | = | 120 | (03/01/93 - 07/01/93) |
| DSC | = | 60 | (07/01/93 - 09/01/93) |
| E | = | 180 | (03/01/93 - 09/01/93) |
| M | = | 2 | (semi-annual) |
| N | = | 60 | (07/01/93 - 03/01/23) |
| R | = | 0.050000 | (5.0000%) |
| RV | = | 100.0000 | |
| Y | = | 0.060000 | (6.0000%) |

### Result:
| | | |
|---|---|---|
| Price | = | 86.210 |
| Accrued interest | = | 2.50 |

Note: These results are calculated useing M.S.R.B. Rule G–33 in which odd first and/or odd last periods are ignored in calculating price/yield. The accrued interest however, is based on the actual number of days accrued.

## BENCHMARK # 11D

Corporate Bond
| | | |
|---|---|---|
| Settlement date | 07/01/93 |
| Maturity date | 03/01/23 |
| Issue/dated date | 01/01/93 |
| First coupon date | 09/01/93 |
| Day count basis | 30/360 |

### Definition of Variables (Formula 9)

| | | | |
|---|---|---|---|
| A1 | = | 60 | (01/01/93 - 03/01/93) |
| A2 | = | 120 | (03/01/93 - 07/01/93) |
| DFC1 | = | 60 | (01/01/93 - 03/01/93) |
| DFC2 | = | 180 | (03/01/93 - 09/01/93) |
| DSC | = | 60 | (07/01/93 - 09/01/93) |
| E | = | 180 | (03/01/93 - 09/01/93) |
| M | = | 2 | (semi-annual) |
| N | = | 59 | (09/01/93 - 03/01/23) |
| NCF | = | 2 | (01/01/93 - 09/01/93) |
| $NLF_1$ | = | 180 | (09/01/92 - 03/01/93) |
| $NLF_2$ | = | 180 | (03/01/93 - 09/01/93) |
| Nqf | = | 0 | (07/01/93 - 09/01/93) |
| R | = | 0.050000 | (5.0000%) |
| RV | = | 100.0000 | |
| Y | = | 0.060000 | (6.0000%) |

### Result:
| | | |
|---|---|---|
| Price | = | 86.202 |
| Accrued interest | = | 2.50 |

## BENCHMARK # 12A

Treasury Bond
| | |
|---|---|
| Settlement date | 07/01/93 |
| Maturity date | 03/01/23 |
| Issue/dated date | 06/01/93 |
| First coupon date | 09/01/93 |
| Day count basis | Actual/Actual |

**Definition of Variables (Formula 8)**

| | | | |
|---|---|---|---|
| A | = | 30 | (06/01/93 - 07/01/93) |
| DFC | = | 92 | (06/01/93 - 09/01/93) |
| DSC | = | 62 | (07/01/93 - 09/01/93) |
| E | = | 184 | (03/01/93 - 09/01/93) |
| M | = | 2 | (semi-annual) |
| N | = | 60 | (07/01/93 - 03/01/23) |
| R | = | 0.050000 | (5.0000%) |
| RV | = | 100.0000 | |
| Y | = | 0.040000 | (4.0000%) |

**Result:**

| | | |
|---|---|---|
| Price | = | 117.282516 |
| Accrued interest | = | 0.41 |

## BENCHMARK # 12B

Agency Bond
| | |
|---|---|
| Settlement date | 07/01/93 |
| Maturity date | 03/01/23 |
| Issue/dated date | 06/01/93 |
| First coupon date | 09/01/93 |
| Day count basis | 30/360 |

**Definition of Variables (Formula 8)**

| | | | |
|---|---|---|---|
| A | = | 30 | (06/01/93 - 07/01/93) |
| DFC | = | 90 | (06/01/93 - 09/01/93) |
| DSC | = | 60 | (07/01/93 - 09/01/93) |
| E | = | 180 | (03/01/93 - 09/01/93) |
| M | = | 2 | (semi-annual) |
| N | = | 60 | (07/01/93 - 03/01/23) |
| R | = | 0.050000 | (5.0000%) |
| RV | = | 100.0000 | |
| Y | = | 0.040000 | (4.0000%) |

**Result:**

| | | |
|---|---|---|
| Price | = | 117.281902 |
| Accrued interest | = | 0.42 |

## BENCHMARK # 12C

Municipal Bond
| | |
|---|---|
| Settlement date | 07/01/93 |
| Maturity date | 03/01/23 |
| Issue/dated date | 06/01/93 |
| First coupon date | 09/01/93 |
| Day count basis | 30/360 |

**Definition of Variables (Formula 7)**

| | | | |
|---|---|---|---|
| A | = | 120 | (03/01/93 - 07/01/93) |
| DSC | = | 60 | (07/01/93 - 09/01/93) |
| E | = | 180 | (03/01/93 - 09/01/93) |
| M | = | 2 | (semi-annual) |
| N | = | 60 | (07/01/93 - 03/01/23) |
| R | = | 0.050000 | (5.0000%) |
| RV | = | 100.0000 | |
| Y | = | 0.040000 | (4.0000%) |

**Result:**

| | | |
|---|---|---|
| Price | = | 117.273 |
| Accrued interest | = | 0.42 |

Note: These results are calculated useing M.S.R.B. Rule
G–33 in which odd first and/or odd last periods
are ignored in calculating price/yield. The
accrued interest however, is based on the actual
number of days accrued.

## BENCHMARK # 12D

Corporate Bond
| | |
|---|---|
| Settlement date | 07/01/93 |
| Maturity date | 03/01/23 |
| Issue/dated date | 06/01/93 |
| First coupon date | 09/01/93 |
| Day count basis | 30/360 |

**Definition of Variables (Formula 8)**

| | | | |
|---|---|---|---|
| A | = | 30 | (06/01/93 - 07/01/93) |
| DFC | = | 90 | (06/01/93 - 09/01/93) |
| DSC | = | 60 | (07/01/93 - 09/01/93) |
| E | = | 180 | (03/01/93 - 09/01/93) |
| M | = | 2 | (semi-annual) |
| N | = | 60 | (07/01/93 - 03/01/23) |
| R | = | 0.050000 | (5.0000%) |
| RV | = | 100.0000 | |
| Y | = | 0.040000 | (4.0000%) |

**Result:**

| | | |
|---|---|---|
| Price | = | 117.281 |
| Accrued interest | = | 0.42 |

## BENCHMARK # 13A

Treasury Bond
Settlement date 07/15/93
Maturity date 07/15/38
Issue/dated date 07/15/92
First coupon date 01/15/93
Day count basis Actual/Actual

**Definition of Variables (Formula 7)**
A = 0 (07/15/93 - 07/15/93)
DSC = 184 (07/15/93 - 01/15/94)
E = 184 (07/15/93 - 01/15/94)
M = 2 (semi-annual)
N = 90 (07/15/93 - 07/15/38)
R = 0.118750 (11.8750%)
RV = 100.0000
Y = 0.100000 (10.0000%)

**Result:**
Price = 118.517745
Accrued interest = 0.00

## BENCHMARK # 13B

Agency Bond
Settlement date 07/15/93
Maturity date 07/15/38
Issue/dated date 07/15/92
First coupon date 01/15/93
Day count basis 30/360

**Definition of Variables (Formula 7)**
A = 0 (07/15/93 - 07/15/93)
DSC = 180 (07/15/93 - 01/15/94)
E = 180 (07/15/93 - 01/15/94)
M = 2 (semi-annual)
N = 90 (07/15/93 - 07/15/38)
R = 0.118750 (11.8750%)
RV = 100.0000
Y = 0.100000 (10.0000%)

**Result:**
Price = 118.517745
Accrued interest = 0.00

## BENCHMARK # 13C

Municipal Bond
Settlement date 07/15/93
Maturity date 07/15/38
Issue/dated date 07/15/92
First coupon date 01/15/93
Day count basis 30/360

**Definition of Variables (Formula 7)**
A = 0 (07/15/93 - 07/15/93)
DSC = 180 (07/15/93 - 01/15/94)
E = 180 (07/15/93 - 01/15/94)
M = 2 (semi-annual)
N = 90 (07/15/93 - 07/15/38)
R = 0.118750 (11.8750%)
RV = 100.0000
Y = 0.100000 (10.0000%)

**Result:**
Price = 118.517
Accrued interest = 0.00

## BENCHMARK # 13D

Corporate Bond
Settlement date 07/15/93
Maturity date 07/15/38
Issue/dated date 07/15/92
First coupon date 01/15/93
Day count basis 30/360

**Definition of Variables (Formula 7)**
A = 0 (07/15/93 - 07/15/93)
DSC = 180 (07/15/93 - 01/15/94)
E = 180 (07/15/93 - 01/15/94)
M = 2 (semi-annual)
N = 90 (07/15/93 - 07/15/38)
R = 0.118750 (11.8750%)
RV = 100.0000
Y = 0.100000 (10.0000%)

**Result:**
Price = 118.517
Accrued interest = 0.00

## Benchmark # 14a

Treasury Bond
| | |
|---|---|
| Settlement date | 10/26/93 |
| Maturity date | 07/15/38 |
| Issue/dated date | 07/15/92 |
| First coupon date | 01/15/93 |
| Day count basis | Actual/Actual |

**Definition of Variables (Formula 7)**

| | | | |
|---|---|---|---|
| A | = | 103 | (07/15/93 - 10/26/93) |
| DSC | = | 81 | (10/26/93 - 01/15/94) |
| E | = | 184 | (07/15/93 - 01/15/94) |
| M | = | 2 | (semi-annual) |
| N | = | 90 | (10/26/93 - 07/15/38) |
| R | = | 0.118750 | (11.8750%) |
| RV | = | 100.0000 | |
| Y | = | 0.100000 | (10.0000%) |

**Result:**

| | | |
|---|---|---|
| Price | = | 118.475588 |
| Accrued interest | = | 3.32 |

## Benchmark # 14b

Agency Bond
| | |
|---|---|
| Settlement date | 10/26/93 |
| Maturity date | 07/15/38 |
| Issue/dated date | 07/15/92 |
| First coupon date | 01/15/93 |
| Day count basis | 30/360 |

**Definition of Variables (Formula 7)**

| | | | |
|---|---|---|---|
| A | = | 101 | (07/15/93 - 10/26/93) |
| DSC | = | 79 | (10/26/93 - 01/15/94) |
| E | = | 180 | (07/15/93 - 01/15/94) |
| M | = | 2 | (semi-annual) |
| N | = | 90 | (10/26/93 - 07/15/38) |
| R | = | 0.118750 | (11.8750%) |
| RV | = | 100.0000 | |
| Y | = | 0.100000 | (10.0000%) |

**Result:**

| | | |
|---|---|---|
| Price | = | 118.475595 |
| Accrued interest | = | 3.33 |

## Benchmark # 14c

Municipal Bond
| | |
|---|---|
| Settlement date | 10/26/93 |
| Maturity date | 07/15/38 |
| Issue/dated date | 07/15/92 |
| First coupon date | 01/15/93 |
| Day count basis | 30/360 |

**Definition of Variables (Formula 7)**

| | | | |
|---|---|---|---|
| A | = | 101 | (07/15/93 - 10/26/93) |
| DSC | = | 79 | (10/26/93 - 01/15/94) |
| E | = | 180 | (07/15/93 - 01/15/94) |
| M | = | 2 | (semi-annual) |
| N | = | 90 | (10/26/93 - 07/15/38) |
| R | = | 0.118750 | (11.8750%) |
| RV | = | 100.0000 | |
| Y | = | 0.100000 | (10.0000%) |

**Result:**

| | | |
|---|---|---|
| Price | = | 118.475 |
| Accrued interest | = | 3.33 |

## Benchmark # 14d

Corporate Bond
| | |
|---|---|
| Settlement date | 10/26/93 |
| Maturity date | 07/15/38 |
| Issue/dated date | 07/15/92 |
| First coupon date | 01/15/93 |
| Day count basis | 30/360 |

**Definition of Variables (Formula 7)**

| | | | |
|---|---|---|---|
| A | = | 101 | (07/15/93 - 10/26/93) |
| DSC | = | 79 | (10/26/93 - 01/15/94) |
| E | = | 180 | (07/15/93 - 01/15/94) |
| M | = | 2 | (semi-annual) |
| N | = | 90 | (10/26/93 - 07/15/38) |
| R | = | 0.118750 | (11.8750%) |
| RV | = | 100.0000 | |
| Y | = | 0.100000 | (10.0000%) |

**Result:**

| | | |
|---|---|---|
| Price | = | 118.475 |
| Accrued interest | = | 3.33 |

## BENCHMARK # 15A

Treasury Bond
| | |
|---|---|
| Settlement date | 11/01/93 |
| Maturity date | 03/01/94 |
| Issue/dated date | 09/01/73 |
| First coupon date | 03/01/74 |
| Day count basis | Actual/Actual |

**Definition of Variables (Formula 5)**

| | | | |
|---|---|---|---|
| A | = | 61 | (09/01/93 - 11/01/93) |
| DSR | = | 120 | (11/01/93 - 03/01/94) |
| E | = | 181 | (09/01/93 - 03/01/94) |
| M | = | 2 | (semi-annual) |
| P | = | 100.0000 | ($100.0000) |
| R | = | 0.125000 | (12.5000%) |
| RV | = | 100.0000 | |

**Result:**

| | | |
|---|---|---|
| Yield | = | 12.242137 |
| Accrued interest | = | 2.11 |

## BENCHMARK # 15B

Agency Bond
| | |
|---|---|
| Settlement date | 11/01/93 |
| Maturity date | 03/01/94 |
| Issue/dated date | 09/01/73 |
| First coupon date | 03/01/74 |
| Day count basis | 30/360 |

**Definition of Variables (Formula 5)**

| | | | |
|---|---|---|---|
| A | = | 60 | (09/01/93 - 11/01/93) |
| DSR | = | 120 | (11/01/93 - 03/01/94) |
| E | = | 180 | (09/01/93 - 03/01/94) |
| M | = | 2 | (semi-annual) |
| P | = | 100.0000 | ($100.0000) |
| R | = | 0.125000 | (12.5000%) |
| RV | = | 100.0000 | |

**Result:**

| | | |
|---|---|---|
| Yield | = | 12.244898 |
| Accrued interest | = | 2.08 |

## BENCHMARK # 15C

Municipal Bond
| | |
|---|---|
| Settlement date | 11/01/93 |
| Maturity date | 03/01/94 |
| Issue/dated date | 09/01/73 |
| First coupon date | 03/01/74 |
| Day count basis | 30/360 |

**Definition of Variables (Formula 5)**

| | | | |
|---|---|---|---|
| A | = | 60 | (09/01/93 - 11/01/93) |
| DSR | = | 120 | (11/01/93 - 03/01/94) |
| E | = | 180 | (09/01/93 - 03/01/94) |
| M | = | 2 | (semi-annual) |
| P | = | 100.0000 | ($100.0000) |
| R | = | 0.125000 | (12.5000%) |
| RV | = | 100.0000 | |

**Result:**

| | | |
|---|---|---|
| Yield | = | 12.245 |
| Accrued interest | = | 2.08 |

## BENCHMARK # 15D

Corporate Bond
| | |
|---|---|
| Settlement date | 11/01/93 |
| Maturity date | 03/01/94 |
| Issue/dated date | 09/01/73 |
| First coupon date | 03/01/74 |
| Day count basis | 30/360 |

**Definition of Variables (Formula 5)**

| | | | |
|---|---|---|---|
| A | = | 60 | (09/01/93 - 11/01/93) |
| DSR | = | 120 | (11/01/93 - 03/01/94) |
| E | = | 180 | (09/01/93 - 03/01/94) |
| M | = | 2 | (semi-annual) |
| P | = | 100.0000 | ($100.0000) |
| R | = | 0.125000 | (12.5000%) |
| RV | = | 100.0000 | |

**Result:**

| | | |
|---|---|---|
| Yield | = | 12.245 |
| Accrued interest | = | 2.08 |

## BENCHMARK # 16A

Treasury Bond

| | |
|---|---|
| Settlement date | 11/01/93 |
| Maturity date | 03/01/94 |
| Issue/dated date | 09/01/73 |
| First coupon date | 03/01/74 |
| Day count basis | Actual/Actual |

**Definition of Variables (Formula 6)**

| | | | |
|---|---|---|---|
| A | = | 61 | (09/01/93 - 11/01/93) |
| DSR | = | 120 | (11/01/93 - 03/01/94) |
| E | = | 181 | (09/01/93 - 03/01/94) |
| M | = | 2 | (semi-annual) |
| R | = | 0.125000 | (12.5000%) |
| RV | = | 100.0000 | |
| Y | = | 0.100000 | (10.0000%) |

**Result:**

| | | |
|---|---|---|
| Price | = | 100.734555 |
| Accrued interest | = | 2.11 |

## BENCHMARK # 16B

Agency Bond

| | |
|---|---|
| Settlement date | 11/01/93 |
| Maturity date | 03/01/94 |
| Issue/dated date | 09/01/73 |
| First coupon date | 03/01/74 |
| Day count basis | 30/360 |

**Definition of Variables (Formula 6)**

| | | | |
|---|---|---|---|
| A | = | 60 | (09/01/93 - 11/01/93) |
| DSR | = | 120 | (11/01/93 - 03/01/94) |
| E | = | 180 | (09/01/93 - 03/01/94) |
| M | = | 2 | (semi-annual) |
| R | = | 0.125000 | (12.5000%) |
| RV | = | 100.0000 | |
| Y | = | 0.100000 | (10.0000%) |

**Result:**

| | | |
|---|---|---|
| Price | = | 100.739247 |
| Accrued interest | = | 2.08 |

## BENCHMARK # 16C

Municipal Bond

| | |
|---|---|
| Settlement date | 11/01/93 |
| Maturity date | 03/01/94 |
| Issue/dated date | 09/01/73 |
| First coupon date | 03/01/74 |
| Day count basis | 30/360 |

**Definition of Variables (Formula 6)**

| | | | |
|---|---|---|---|
| A | = | 60 | (09/01/93 - 11/01/93) |
| DSR | = | 120 | (11/01/93 - 03/01/94) |
| E | = | 180 | (09/01/93 - 03/01/94) |
| M | = | 2 | (semi-annual) |
| R | = | 0.125000 | (12.5000%) |
| RV | = | 100.0000 | |
| Y | = | 0.100000 | (10.0000%) |

**Result:**

| | | |
|---|---|---|
| Price | = | 100.739 |
| Accrued interest | = | 2.08 |

## BENCHMARK # 16D

Corporate Bond

| | |
|---|---|
| Settlement date | 11/01/93 |
| Maturity date | 03/01/94 |
| Issue/dated date | 09/01/73 |
| First coupon date | 03/01/74 |
| Day count basis | 30/360 |

**Definition of Variables (Formula 6)**

| | | | |
|---|---|---|---|
| A | = | 60 | (09/01/93 - 11/01/93) |
| DSR | = | 120 | (11/01/93 - 03/01/94) |
| E | = | 180 | (09/01/93 - 03/01/94) |
| M | = | 2 | (semi-annual) |
| R | = | 0.125000 | (12.5000%) |
| RV | = | 100.0000 | |
| Y | = | 0.100000 | (10.0000%) |

**Result:**

| | | |
|---|---|---|
| Price | = | 100.739 |
| Accrued interest | = | 2.08 |

## BENCHMARK # 17A

Treasury Bond
Settlement date          06/24/93
Maturity date           01/15/24
Day count basis       Actual/Actual

### Definition of Variables (Formula 7)

| | | | |
|---|---|---|---|
| A | = | 160 | (01/15/93 - 06/24/93) |
| DSC | = | 21 | (06/24/93 - 07/15/93) |
| E | = | 181 | (01/15/93 - 07/15/93) |
| M | = | 2 | (semi-annual) |
| N | = | 62 | (06/24/93 - 01/15/24) |
| R | = | 0.230000 | (23.0000%) |
| RV | = | 100.0000 | |
| Y | = | 0.140000 | (14.0000%) |

**Result:**
Price               =    163.216756
Accrued interest   =    10.17

## BENCHMARK # 17B

Agency Bond
Settlement date          06/24/93
Maturity date           01/15/24
Day count basis       30/360

### Definition of Variables (Formula 7)

| | | | |
|---|---|---|---|
| A | = | 159 | (01/15/93 - 06/24/93) |
| DSC | = | 21 | (06/24/93 - 07/15/93) |
| E | = | 180 | (01/15/93 - 07/15/93) |
| M | = | 2 | (semi-annual) |
| N | = | 62 | (06/24/93 - 01/15/24) |
| R | = | 0.230000 | (23.0000%) |
| RV | = | 100.0000 | |
| Y | = | 0.140000 | (14.0000%) |

**Result:**
Price               =    163.216607
Accrued interest   =    10.16

## BENCHMARK # 17C

Municipal Bond
Settlement date          06/24/93
Maturity date           01/15/24
Day count basis       30/360

### Definition of Variables (Formula 7)

| | | | |
|---|---|---|---|
| A | = | 159 | (01/15/93 - 06/24/93) |
| DSC | = | 21 | (06/24/93 - 07/15/93) |
| E | = | 180 | (01/15/93 - 07/15/93) |
| M | = | 2 | (semi-annual) |
| N | = | 62 | (06/24/93 - 01/15/24) |
| R | = | 0.230000 | (23.0000%) |
| RV | = | 100.0000 | |
| Y | = | 0.140000 | (14.0000%) |

**Result:**
Price               =    163.216
Accrued interest   =    10.16

## BENCHMARK # 17D

Corporate Bond
Settlement date          06/24/93
Maturity date           01/15/24
Day count basis       30/360

### Definition of Variables (Formula 7)

| | | | |
|---|---|---|---|
| A | = | 159 | (01/15/93 - 06/24/93) |
| DSC | = | 21 | (06/24/93 - 07/15/93) |
| E | = | 180 | (01/15/93 - 07/15/93) |
| M | = | 2 | (semi-annual) |
| N | = | 62 | (06/24/93 - 01/15/24) |
| R | = | 0.230000 | (23.0000%) |
| RV | = | 100.0000 | |
| Y | = | 0.140000 | (14.0000%) |

**Result:**
Price               =    163.216
Accrued interest   =    10.16

## BENCHMARK # 18A

Treasury Bond
| | |
|---|---|
| Settlement date | 10/12/92 |
| Maturity date | 06/15/20 |
| Issue/dated date | 08/01/92 |
| First coupon date | 12/31/92 |
| Last coupon date | 12/31/19 |
| Day count basis | Actual/Actual |

### Definition of Variables (Formula 16)

| | | | |
|---|---|---|---|
| A | = | 72 | (08/01/92 - 10/12/92) |
| DFC | = | 152 | (08/01/92 - 12/31/92) |
| DLC | = | 167 | (12/31/19 - 06/15/20) |
| DSC | = | 80 | (10/12/92 - 12/31/92) |
| E | = | 184 | (06/30/92 - 12/31/92) |
| M | = | 2 | (semi-annual) |
| N | = | 55 | (10/12/92 - 12/31/19) |
| NLL | = | 182 | (12/31/19 - 06/30/20) |
| R | = | 0.057500 | (5.7500%) |
| RV | = | 100.0000 | |
| Y | = | 0.065000 | (6.5000%) |

**Result:**
| | | |
|---|---|---|
| Price | = | 90.422798 |
| Accrued interest | = | 1.13 |

## BENCHMARK # 18B

Agency Bond
| | |
|---|---|
| Settlement date | 10/12/92 |
| Maturity date | 06/15/20 |
| Issue/dated date | 08/01/92 |
| First coupon date | 12/31/92 |
| Last coupon date | 12/31/19 |
| Day count basis | 30/360 |

### Definition of Variables (Formula 16)

| | | | |
|---|---|---|---|
| A | = | 71 | (08/01/92 - 10/12/92) |
| DFC | = | 150 | (08/01/92 - 12/31/92) |
| DLC | = | 165 | (12/31/19 - 06/15/20) |
| DSC | = | 79 | (10/12/92 - 12/31/92) |
| E | = | 180 | (06/30/92 - 12/31/92) |
| M | = | 2 | (semi-annual) |
| N | = | 55 | (10/12/92 - 12/31/19) |
| NLL | = | 180 | (12/31/19 - 06/30/20) |
| R | = | 0.057500 | (5.7500%) |
| RV | = | 100.0000 | |
| Y | = | 0.065000 | (6.5000%) |

**Result:**
| | | |
|---|---|---|
| Price | = | 90.422909 |
| Accrued interest | = | 1.13 |

## BENCHMARK # 18C

Municipal Bond
| | |
|---|---|
| Settlement date | 10/12/92 |
| Maturity date | 06/15/20 |
| Issue/dated date | 08/01/92 |
| First coupon date | 12/31/92 |
| Last coupon date | 12/15/19 |
| Day count basis | 30/360 |

### Definition of Variables (Formula 7)

| | | | |
|---|---|---|---|
| A | = | 117 | (06/15/92 - 10/12/92) |
| DSC | = | 63 | (10/12/92 - 12/15/92) |
| E | = | 180 | (06/15/92 - 12/15/92) |
| M | = | 2 | (semi-annual) |
| N | = | 56 | (10/12/92 - 06/15/20) |
| R | = | 0.057500 | (5.7500%) |
| RV | = | 100.0000 | |
| Y | = | 0.065000 | (6.5000%) |

**Result:**
| | | |
|---|---|---|
| Price | = | 90.415 |
| Accrued interest | = | 1.13 |

Note: These results are calculated useing M.S.R.B. Rule G–33 in which odd first and/or odd last periods are ignored in calculating price/yield. The accrued interest however, is based on the actual number of days accrued.

## BENCHMARK # 18D

Corporate Bond
| | |
|---|---|
| Settlement date | 10/12/92 |
| Maturity date | 06/15/20 |
| Issue/dated date | 08/01/92 |
| First coupon date | 12/31/92 |
| Last coupon date | 12/31/19 |
| Day count basis | 30/360 |

### Definition of Variables (Formula 16)

| | | | |
|---|---|---|---|
| A | = | 71 | (08/01/92 - 10/12/92) |
| DFC | = | 150 | (08/01/92 - 12/31/92) |
| DLC | = | 165 | (12/31/19 - 06/15/20) |
| DSC | = | 79 | (10/12/92 - 12/31/92) |
| E | = | 180 | (06/30/92 - 12/31/92) |
| M | = | 2 | (semi-annual) |
| N | = | 55 | (10/12/92 - 12/31/19) |
| NLL | = | 180 | (12/31/19 - 06/30/20) |
| R | = | 0.057500 | (5.7500%) |
| RV | = | 100.0000 | |
| Y | = | 0.065000 | (6.5000%) |

**Result:**
| | | |
|---|---|---|
| Price | = | 90.422 |
| Accrued interest | = | 1.13 |

## BENCHMARK # 19A

Treasury Bond
| | |
|---|---|
| Settlement date | 07/15/92 |
| Maturity date | 11/15/92 |
| Last coupon date | 06/01/92 |
| Day count basis | Actual/Actual |

**Definition of Variables (Formula 11)**

| | | | |
|---|---|---|---|
| A | = | 44 | (06/01/92 - 07/15/92) |
| DLC | = | 167 | (06/01/92 - 11/15/92) |
| DSR | = | 123 | (07/15/92 - 12/01/92) |
| E | = | 183 | (06/01/92 - 12/01/92) |
| M | = | 2 | (semi-annual) |
| R | = | 0.101220 | (10.1220%) |
| RV | = | 100.0000 | |
| Y | = | 0.033750 | (3.3750%) |

**Result:**

| | | |
|---|---|---|
| Price | = | 102.216456 |
| Accrued interest | = | 1.21 |

## BENCHMARK # 19B

Agency Bond
| | |
|---|---|
| Settlement date | 07/15/92 |
| Maturity date | 11/15/92 |
| Last coupon date | 06/01/92 |
| Day count basis | 30/360 |

**Definition of Variables (Formula 11)**

| | | | |
|---|---|---|---|
| A | = | 44 | (06/01/92 - 07/15/92) |
| DLC | = | 164 | (06/01/92 - 11/15/92) |
| DSR | = | 120 | (07/15/92 - 12/01/92) |
| E | = | 180 | (06/01/92 - 12/01/92) |
| M | = | 2 | (semi-annual) |
| R | = | 0.101220 | (10.1220%) |
| RV | = | 100.0000 | |
| Y | = | 0.033750 | (3.3750%) |

**Result:**

| | | |
|---|---|---|
| Price | = | 102.210217 |
| Accrued interest | = | 1.24 |

## BENCHMARK # 19C

Municipal Bond
| | |
|---|---|
| Settlement date | 07/15/92 |
| Maturity date | 11/15/92 |
| Last coupon date | 05/15/92 |
| Day count basis | 30/360 |

**Definition of Variables (Formula 6)**

| | | | |
|---|---|---|---|
| A | = | 60 | (05/15/92 - 07/15/92) |
| DSR | = | 120 | (07/15/92 - 11/15/92) |
| E | = | 180 | (05/15/92 - 11/15/92) |
| M | = | 2 | (semi-annual) |
| R | = | 0.101220 | (10.1220%) |
| RV | = | 100.0000 | |
| Y | = | 0.033750 | (3.3750%) |

**Result:**

| | | |
|---|---|---|
| Price | = | 102.205 |
| Accrued interest | = | 1.24 |

Note: These results are calculated useing M.S.R.B. Rule G–33 in which odd first and/or odd last periods are ignored in calculating price/yield. The accrued interest however, is based on the actual number of days accrued.

## BENCHMARK # 19D

Corporate Bond
| | |
|---|---|
| Settlement date | 07/15/92 |
| Maturity date | 11/15/92 |
| Last coupon date | 06/01/92 |
| Day count basis | 30/360 |

**Definition of Variables (Formula 11)**

| | | | |
|---|---|---|---|
| A | = | 44 | (06/01/92 - 07/15/92) |
| DLC | = | 164 | (06/01/92 - 11/15/92) |
| DSR | = | 120 | (07/15/92 - 12/01/92) |
| E | = | 180 | (06/01/92 - 12/01/92) |
| M | = | 2 | (semi-annual) |
| R | = | 0.101220 | (10.1220%) |
| RV | = | 100.0000 | |
| Y | = | 0.033750 | (3.3750%) |

**Result:**

| | | |
|---|---|---|
| Price | = | 102.210 |
| Accrued interest | = | 1.24 |

## Benchmark # 20A

Treasury Bond
Settlement date 07/15/92
Maturity date 11/15/92
Last coupon date 06/01/92
Day count basis Actual/Actual

### Definition of Variables (Formula 10)

| | | | |
|---|---|---|---|
| A | = | 44 | (06/01/92 - 07/15/92) |
| DLC | = | 167 | (06/01/92 - 11/15/92) |
| DSR | = | 123 | (07/15/92 - 12/01/92) |
| E | = | 183 | (06/01/92 - 12/01/92) |
| M | = | 2 | (semi-annual) |
| P | = | 98.7500 | ($98.7500) |
| R | = | 0.101220 | (10.1220%) |
| RV | = | 100.0000 | |

### Result:

Yield = 13.867351
Accrued interest = 1.21

## Benchmark # 20B

Agency Bond
Settlement date 07/15/92
Maturity date 11/15/92
Last coupon date 06/01/92
Day count basis 30/360

### Definition of Variables (Formula 10)

| | | | |
|---|---|---|---|
| A | = | 44 | (06/01/92 - 07/15/92) |
| DLC | = | 164 | (06/01/92 - 11/15/92) |
| DSR | = | 120 | (07/15/92 - 12/01/92) |
| E | = | 180 | (06/01/92 - 12/01/92) |
| M | = | 2 | (semi-annual) |
| P | = | 98.7500 | ($98.7500) |
| R | = | 0.101220 | (10.1220%) |
| RV | = | 100.0000 | |

### Result:

Yield = 13.873785
Accrued interest = 1.24

## Benchmark # 20C

Municipal Bond
Settlement date 07/15/92
Maturity date 11/15/92
Last coupon date 05/15/92
Day count basis 30/360

### Definition of Variables (Formula 5)

| | | | |
|---|---|---|---|
| A | = | 60 | (05/15/92 - 07/15/92) |
| DSR | = | 120 | (07/15/92 - 11/15/92) |
| E | = | 180 | (05/15/92 - 11/15/92) |
| M | = | 2 | (semi-annual) |
| P | = | 98.7500 | ($98.7500) |
| R | = | 0.101220 | (10.1220%) |
| RV | = | 100.0000 | |

### Result:

Yield = 13.812
Accrued interest = 1.24

Note: These results are calculated useing M.S.R.B. Rule G–33 in which odd first and/or odd last periods are ignored in calculating price/yield. The accrued interest however, is based on the actual number of days accrued.

## Benchmark # 20D

Corporate Bond
Settlement date 07/15/92
Maturity date 11/15/92
Last coupon date 06/01/92
Day count basis 30/360

### Definition of Variables (Formula 10)

| | | | |
|---|---|---|---|
| A | = | 44 | (06/01/92 - 07/15/92) |
| DLC | = | 164 | (06/01/92 - 11/15/92) |
| DSR | = | 120 | (07/15/92 - 12/01/92) |
| E | = | 180 | (06/01/92 - 12/01/92) |
| M | = | 2 | (semi-annual) |
| P | = | 98.7500 | ($98.7500) |
| R | = | 0.101220 | (10.1220%) |
| RV | = | 100.0000 | |

### Result:

Yield = 13.874
Accrued interest = 1.24

## Benchmark # 21A

Treasury Bond
| | |
|---|---|
| Settlement date | 10/12/92 |
| Maturity date | 11/15/92 |
| Last coupon date | 02/01/92 |
| Day count basis | Actual/Actual |

### Definition of Variables (Formula 13)

| | | | |
|---|---|---|---|
| $A1$ | = | 182 | (02/01/92 - 08/01/92) |
| $A2$ | = | 72 | (08/01/92 - 10/12/92) |
| $DLC_1$ | = | 182 | (02/01/92 - 08/01/92) |
| $DLC_2$ | = | 106 | (08/01/92 - 11/15/92) |
| $DSC_1$ | = | 0 | (N/A) |
| $DSC_2$ | = | 34 | (10/12/92 - 11/15/92) |
| $M$ | = | 2 | (semi-annual) |
| $NCL$ | = | 2 | (02/01/92 - 11/15/92) |
| $NLL_1$ | = | 182 | (02/01/92 - 08/01/92) |
| $NLL_2$ | = | 184 | (08/01/92 - 02/01/93) |
| $R$ | = | 0.122500 | (12.2500%) |
| $RV$ | = | 100.0000 | |
| $Y$ | = | 0.033750 | (3.3750%) |

**Result:**

| | | |
|---|---|---|
| Price | = | 100.791023 |
| Accrued interest | = | 8.49 |

## Benchmark # 21B

Agency Bond
| | |
|---|---|
| Settlement date | 10/12/92 |
| Maturity date | 11/15/92 |
| Last coupon date | 02/01/92 |
| Day count basis | 30/360 |

### Definition of Variables (Formula 13)

| | | | |
|---|---|---|---|
| $A1$ | = | 180 | (02/01/92 - 08/01/92) |
| $A2$ | = | 71 | (08/01/92 - 10/12/92) |
| $DLC_1$ | = | 180 | (02/01/92 - 08/01/92) |
| $DLC_2$ | = | 104 | (08/01/92 - 11/15/92) |
| $DSC_1$ | = | 0 | (N/A) |
| $DSC_2$ | = | 33 | (10/12/92 - 11/15/92) |
| $M$ | = | 2 | (semi-annual) |
| $NCL$ | = | 2 | (02/01/92 - 11/15/92) |
| $NLL_1$ | = | 180 | (02/01/92 - 08/01/92) |
| $NLL_2$ | = | 180 | (08/01/92 - 02/01/93) |
| $R$ | = | 0.122500 | (12.2500%) |
| $RV$ | = | 100.0000 | |
| $Y$ | = | 0.033750 | (3.3750%) |

**Result:**

| | | |
|---|---|---|
| Price | = | 100.784690 |
| Accrued interest | = | 8.54 |

## Benchmark # 21C

Municipal Bond
| | |
|---|---|
| Settlement date | 10/12/92 |
| Maturity date | 11/15/92 |
| Last coupon date | 05/15/92 |
| Day count basis | 30/360 |

### Definition of Variables (Formula 6)

| | | | |
|---|---|---|---|
| $A$ | = | 147 | (05/15/92 - 10/12/92) |
| $DSR$ | = | 33 | (10/12/92 - 11/15/92) |
| $E$ | = | 180 | (05/15/92 - 11/15/92) |
| $M$ | = | 2 | (semi-annual) |
| $R$ | = | 0.122500 | (12.2500%) |
| $RV$ | = | 100.0000 | |
| $Y$ | = | 0.033750 | (3.3750%) |

**Result:**

| | | |
|---|---|---|
| Price | = | 100.795 |
| Accrued interest | = | 8.54 |

Note: These results are calculated useing M.S.R.B. Rule G–33 in which odd first and/or odd last periods are ignored in calculating price/yield. The accrued interest however, is based on the actual number of days accrued.

## Benchmark # 21D

Corporate Bond
| | |
|---|---|
| Settlement date | 10/12/92 |
| Maturity date | 11/15/92 |
| Last coupon date | 02/01/92 |
| Day count basis | 30/360 |

### Definition of Variables (Formula 13)

| | | | |
|---|---|---|---|
| $A1$ | = | 180 | (02/01/92 - 08/01/92) |
| $A2$ | = | 71 | (08/01/92 - 10/12/92) |
| $DLC_1$ | = | 180 | (02/01/92 - 08/01/92) |
| $DLC_2$ | = | 104 | (08/01/92 - 11/15/92) |
| $DSC_1$ | = | 0 | (N/A) |
| $DSC_2$ | = | 33 | (10/12/92 - 11/15/92) |
| $M$ | = | 2 | (semi-annual) |
| $NCL$ | = | 2 | (02/01/92 - 11/15/92) |
| $NLL_1$ | = | 180 | (02/01/92 - 08/01/92) |
| $NLL_2$ | = | 180 | (08/01/92 - 02/01/93) |
| $R$ | = | 0.122500 | (12.2500%) |
| $RV$ | = | 100.0000 | |
| $Y$ | = | 0.033750 | (3.3750%) |

**Result:**

| | | |
|---|---|---|
| Price | = | 100.784 |
| Accrued interest | = | 8.54 |

## BENCHMARK # 22A

Treasury Bond
Settlement date      10/12/92
Maturity date      11/15/92
Last coupon date      02/01/92
Day count basis      Actual/Actual

### Definition of Variables (Formula 12)

| | | | |
|---|---|---|---|
| $A1$ | = | 182 | (02/01/92 - 08/01/92) |
| $A2$ | = | 72 | (08/01/92 - 10/12/92) |
| $DLC_1$ | = | 182 | (02/01/92 - 08/01/92) |
| $DLC_2$ | = | 106 | (08/01/92 - 11/15/92) |
| $DSC_1$ | = | 0 | (N/A) |
| $DSC_2$ | = | 34 | (10/12/92 - 11/15/92) |
| $M$ | = | 2 | (semi-annual) |
| $NCL$ | = | 2 | (02/01/92 - 11/15/92) |
| $NLL_1$ | = | 182 | (02/01/92 - 08/01/92) |
| $NLL_2$ | = | 184 | (08/01/92 - 02/01/93) |
| $P$ | = | 101.0000 | ($101.0000) |
| $R$ | = | 0.122500 | (12.2500%) |
| $RV$ | = | 100.0000 | |

**Result:**
Yield      =      1.302794
Accrued interest    =      8.49

## BENCHMARK # 22B

Agency Bond
Settlement date      10/12/92
Maturity date      11/15/92
Last coupon date      02/01/92
Day count basis      30/360

### Definition of Variables (Formula 12)

| | | | |
|---|---|---|---|
| $A1$ | = | 180 | (02/01/92 - 08/01/92) |
| $A2$ | = | 71 | (08/01/92 - 10/12/92) |
| $DLC_1$ | = | 180 | (02/01/92 - 08/01/92) |
| $DLC_2$ | = | 104 | (08/01/92 - 11/15/92) |
| $DSC_1$ | = | 0 | (N/A) |
| $DSC_2$ | = | 33 | (10/12/92 - 11/15/92) |
| $M$ | = | 2 | (semi-annual) |
| $NCL$ | = | 2 | (02/01/92 - 11/15/92) |
| $NLL_1$ | = | 180 | (02/01/92 - 08/01/92) |
| $NLL_2$ | = | 180 | (08/01/92 - 02/01/93) |
| $P$ | = | 101.0000 | ($101.0000) |
| $R$ | = | 0.122500 | (12.2500%) |
| $RV$ | = | 100.0000 | |

**Result:**
Yield      =      1.224116
Accrued interest    =      8.54

## BENCHMARK # 22C

Municipal Bond
Settlement date      10/12/92
Maturity date      11/15/92
Last coupon date      05/15/92
Day count basis      30/360

### Definition of Variables (Formula 5)

| | | | |
|---|---|---|---|
| $A$ | = | 147 | (05/15/92 - 10/12/92) |
| $DSR$ | = | 33 | (10/12/92 - 11/15/92) |
| $E$ | = | 180 | (05/15/92 - 11/15/92) |
| $M$ | = | 2 | (semi-annual) |
| $P$ | = | 101.0000 | ($101.0000) |
| $R$ | = | 0.122500 | (12.2500%) |
| $RV$ | = | 100.0000 | |

**Result:**
Yield      =      1.265
Accrued interest    =      8.54

Note: These results are calculated useing M.S.R.B. Rule
G–33 in which odd first and/or odd last periods
are ignored in calculating price/yield. The
accrued interest however, is based on the actual
number of days accrued.

## BENCHMARK # 22D

Corporate Bond
Settlement date      10/12/92
Maturity date      11/15/92
Last coupon date      02/01/92
Day count basis      30/360

### Definition of Variables (Formula 12)

| | | | |
|---|---|---|---|
| $A1$ | = | 180 | (02/01/92 - 08/01/92) |
| $A2$ | = | 71 | (08/01/92 - 10/12/92) |
| $DLC_1$ | = | 180 | (02/01/92 - 08/01/92) |
| $DLC_2$ | = | 104 | (08/01/92 - 11/15/92) |
| $DSC_1$ | = | 0 | (N/A) |
| $DSC_2$ | = | 33 | (10/12/92 - 11/15/92) |
| $M$ | = | 2 | (semi-annual) |
| $NCL$ | = | 2 | (02/01/92 - 11/15/92) |
| $NLL_1$ | = | 180 | (02/01/92 - 08/01/92) |
| $NLL_2$ | = | 180 | (08/01/92 - 02/01/93) |
| $P$ | = | 101.0000 | ($101.0000) |
| $R$ | = | 0.122500 | (12.2500%) |
| $RV$ | = | 100.0000 | |

**Result:**
Yield      =      1.224
Accrued interest    =      8.54

## Benchmark # 23A

Treasury Bond
Settlement date       03/12/92
Maturity date       11/15/92
Last coupon date       02/01/92
Day count basis       Actual/Actual

**Definition of Variables (Formula 13)**

| | | | |
|---|---|---|---|
| $A1$ | = | 40 | (02/01/92 - 03/12/92) |
| $A2$ | = | 0 | |
| $DLC_1$ | = | 182 | (02/01/92 - 08/01/92) |
| $DLC_2$ | = | 106 | (08/01/92 - 11/15/92) |
| $DSC_1$ | = | 142 | (03/12/92 - 08/01/92) |
| $DSC_2$ | = | 106 | (08/01/92 - 11/15/92) |
| $M$ | = | 2 | (semi-annual) |
| $NCL$ | = | 2 | (02/01/92 - 11/15/92) |
| $NLL_1$ | = | 182 | (02/01/92 - 08/01/92) |
| $NLL_2$ | = | 184 | (08/01/92 - 02/01/93) |
| $R$ | = | 0.122500 | (12.2500%) |
| $RV$ | = | 100.0000 | |
| $Y$ | = | 0.033750 | (3.3750%) |

**Result:**
Price       = 105.834163
Accrued interest    =    1.35

## Benchmark # 23B

Agency Bond
Settlement date       03/12/92
Maturity date       11/15/92
Last coupon date       02/01/92
Day count basis       30/360

**Definition of Variables (Formula 13)**

| | | | |
|---|---|---|---|
| $A1$ | = | 41 | (02/01/92 - 03/12/92) |
| $A2$ | = | 0 | |
| $DLC_1$ | = | 180 | (02/01/92 - 08/01/92) |
| $DLC_2$ | = | 104 | (08/01/92 - 11/15/92) |
| $DSC_1$ | = | 139 | (03/12/92 - 08/01/92) |
| $DSC_2$ | = | 104 | (08/01/92 - 11/15/92) |
| $M$ | = | 2 | (semi-annual) |
| $NCL$ | = | 2 | (02/01/92 - 11/15/92) |
| $NLL_1$ | = | 180 | (02/01/92 - 08/01/92) |
| $NLL_2$ | = | 180 | (08/01/92 - 02/01/93) |
| $R$ | = | 0.122500 | (12.2500%) |
| $RV$ | = | 100.0000 | |
| $Y$ | = | 0.033750 | (3.3750%) |

**Result:**
Price       = 105.826116
Accrued interest    =    1.40

## Benchmark # 23C

Municipal Bond
Settlement date       03/12/92
Maturity date       11/15/92
Last coupon date       05/15/92
Day count basis       30/360

**Definition of Variables (Formula 7)**

| | | | |
|---|---|---|---|
| $A$ | = | 117 | (11/15/91 - 03/12/92) |
| $DSC$ | = | 63 | (03/12/92 - 05/15/92) |
| $E$ | = | 180 | (11/15/91 - 05/15/92) |
| $M$ | = | 2 | (semi-annual) |
| $N$ | = | 2 | (03/12/92 - 11/15/92) |
| $R$ | = | 0.122500 | (12.2500%) |
| $RV$ | = | 100.0000 | |
| $Y$ | = | 0.033750 | (3.3750%) |

**Result:**
Price       = 105.862
Accrued interest    =    1.40

Note: These results are calculated useing M.S.R.B. Rule G–33 in which odd first and/or odd last periods are ignored in calculating price/yield. The accrued interest however, is based on the actual number of days accrued.

## Benchmark # 23D

Corporate Bond
Settlement date       03/12/92
Maturity date       11/15/92
Last coupon date       02/01/92
Day count basis       30/360

**Definition of Variables (Formula 13)**

| | | | |
|---|---|---|---|
| $A1$ | = | 41 | (02/01/92 - 03/12/92) |
| $A2$ | = | 0 | |
| $DLC_1$ | = | 180 | (02/01/92 - 08/01/92) |
| $DLC_2$ | = | 104 | (08/01/92 - 11/15/92) |
| $DSC_1$ | = | 139 | (03/12/92 - 08/01/92) |
| $DSC_2$ | = | 104 | (08/01/92 - 11/15/92) |
| $M$ | = | 2 | (semi-annual) |
| $NCL$ | = | 2 | (02/01/92 - 11/15/92) |
| $NLL_1$ | = | 180 | (02/01/92 - 08/01/92) |
| $NLL_2$ | = | 180 | (08/01/92 - 02/01/93) |
| $R$ | = | 0.122500 | (12.2500%) |
| $RV$ | = | 100.0000 | |
| $Y$ | = | 0.033750 | (3.3750%) |

**Result:**
Price       = 105.826
Accrued interest    =    1.40

## Benchmark # 24A

Treasury Bond
| | | |
|---|---|---|
| Settlement date | | 03/12/92 |
| Maturity date | | 11/15/92 |
| Last coupon date | | 02/01/92 |
| Day count basis | | Actual/Actual |

### Definition of Variables (Formula 12)

| | | | |
|---|---|---|---|
| $A_1$ | = | 40 | (02/01/92 - 03/12/92) |
| $A_2$ | = | 0 | |
| $DLC_1$ | = | 182 | (02/01/92 - 08/01/92) |
| $DLC_2$ | = | 106 | (08/01/92 - 11/15/92) |
| $DSC_1$ | = | 142 | (03/12/92 - 08/01/92) |
| $DSC_2$ | = | 106 | (08/01/92 - 11/15/92) |
| $M$ | = | 2 | (semi-annual) |
| $NCL$ | = | 2 | (02/01/92 - 11/15/92) |
| $NLL_1$ | = | 182 | (02/01/92 - 08/01/92) |
| $NLL_2$ | = | 184 | (08/01/92 - 02/01/93) |
| $P$ | = | 101.0000 | ($101.0000) |
| $R$ | = | 0.122500 | (12.2500%) |
| $RV$ | = | 100.0000 | |

### Result:
| | | |
|---|---|---|
| Yield | = | 10.523429 |
| Accrued interest | = | 1.35 |

## Benchmark # 24B

Agency Bond
| | | |
|---|---|---|
| Settlement date | | 03/12/92 |
| Maturity date | | 11/15/92 |
| Last coupon date | | 02/01/92 |
| Day count basis | | 30/360 |

### Definition of Variables (Formula 12)

| | | | |
|---|---|---|---|
| $A_1$ | = | 41 | (02/01/92 - 03/12/92) |
| $A_2$ | = | 0 | |
| $DLC_1$ | = | 180 | (02/01/92 - 08/01/92) |
| $DLC_2$ | = | 104 | (08/01/92 - 11/15/92) |
| $DSC_1$ | = | 139 | (03/12/92 - 08/01/92) |
| $DSC_2$ | = | 104 | (08/01/92 - 11/15/92) |
| $M$ | = | 2 | (semi-annual) |
| $NCL$ | = | 2 | (02/01/92 - 11/15/92) |
| $NLL_1$ | = | 180 | (02/01/92 - 08/01/92) |
| $NLL_2$ | = | 180 | (08/01/92 - 02/01/93) |
| $P$ | = | 101.0000 | ($101.0000) |
| $R$ | = | 0.122500 | (12.2500%) |
| $RV$ | = | 100.0000 | |

### Result:
| | | |
|---|---|---|
| Yield | = | 10.516631 |
| Accrued interest | = | 1.40 |

## Benchmark # 24C

Municipal Bond
| | | |
|---|---|---|
| Settlement date | | 03/12/92 |
| Maturity date | | 11/15/92 |
| Last coupon date | | 02/01/92 |
| Day count basis | | 30/360 |

### No Formula

Note: Since municipal securities must follow M.S.R.B. Rule G–33, in which odd first and/or odd last periods are ignored in calculating price/yield, the example above would create a situation with more than one period to maturity. There is no formula for this situation and an iterative method must be used to solve for yield. The answer given below uses such a method in conjunction with Formula 7.

### Result:
| | | |
|---|---|---|
| Yield | = | 10.621 |
| Accrued interest | = | 1.40 |

## Benchmark # 24D

Corporate Bond
| | | |
|---|---|---|
| Settlement date | | 03/12/92 |
| Maturity date | | 11/15/92 |
| Last coupon date | | 02/01/92 |
| Day count basis | | 30/360 |

### Definition of Variables (Formula 12)

| | | | |
|---|---|---|---|
| $A_1$ | = | 41 | (02/01/92 - 03/12/92) |
| $A_2$ | = | 0 | |
| $DLC_1$ | = | 180 | (02/01/92 - 08/01/92) |
| $DLC_2$ | = | 104 | (08/01/92 - 11/15/92) |
| $DSC_1$ | = | 139 | (03/12/92 - 08/01/92) |
| $DSC_2$ | = | 104 | (08/01/92 - 11/15/92) |
| $M$ | = | 2 | (semi-annual) |
| $NCL$ | = | 2 | (02/01/92 - 11/15/92) |
| $NLL_1$ | = | 180 | (02/01/92 - 08/01/92) |
| $NLL_2$ | = | 180 | (08/01/92 - 02/01/93) |
| $P$ | = | 101.0000 | ($101.0000) |
| $R$ | = | 0.122500 | (12.2500%) |
| $RV$ | = | 100.0000 | |

### Result:
| | | |
|---|---|---|
| Yield | = | 10.517 |
| Accrued interest | = | 1.40 |

## BENCHMARK # 25A

Treasury Bond
| | | |
|---|---|---|
| Settlement date | | 10/12/92 |
| Maturity date | | 09/15/20 |
| Last coupon date | | 06/15/20 |
| Day count basis | | Actual/Actual |

**Definition of Variables (Formula 14)**
| | | | |
|---|---|---|---|
| A | = | 119 | (06/15/92 - 10/12/92) |
| DLC | = | 92 | (06/15/20 - 09/15/20) |
| DSC | = | 64 | (10/12/92 - 12/15/92) |
| E | = | 183 | (06/15/92 - 12/15/92) |
| M | = | 2 | (semi-annual) |
| N | = | 56 | (10/12/92 - 06/15/20) |
| NLL | = | 183 | (06/15/20 - 12/15/20) |
| R | = | 0.057500 | (5.7500%) |
| RV | = | 100.0000 | |
| Y | = | 0.075000 | (7.5000%) |

**Result:**
| | | |
|---|---|---|
| Price | = | 79.641998 |
| Accrued interest | = | 1.87 |

## BENCHMARK # 25B

Agency Bond
| | | |
|---|---|---|
| Settlement date | | 10/12/92 |
| Maturity date | | 09/15/20 |
| Last coupon date | | 06/15/20 |
| Day count basis | | 30/360 |

**Definition of Variables (Formula 14)**
| | | | |
|---|---|---|---|
| A | = | 117 | (06/15/92 - 10/12/92) |
| DLC | = | 90 | (06/15/20 - 09/15/20) |
| DSC | = | 63 | (10/12/92 - 12/15/92) |
| E | = | 180 | (06/15/92 - 12/15/92) |
| M | = | 2 | (semi-annual) |
| N | = | 56 | (10/12/92 - 06/15/20) |
| NLL | = | 180 | (06/15/20 - 12/15/20) |
| R | = | 0.057500 | (5.7500%) |
| RV | = | 100.0000 | |
| Y | = | 0.075000 | (7.5000%) |

**Result:**
| | | |
|---|---|---|
| Price | = | 79.641963 |
| Accrued interest | = | 1.87 |

## BENCHMARK # 25C

Municipal Bond
| | | |
|---|---|---|
| Settlement date | | 10/12/92 |
| Maturity date | | 09/15/20 |
| Last coupon date | | 03/15/20 |
| Day count basis | | 30/360 |

**Definition of Variables (Formula 7)**
| | | | |
|---|---|---|---|
| A | = | 27 | (09/15/92 - 10/12/92) |
| DSC | = | 153 | (10/12/92 - 03/15/93) |
| E | = | 180 | (09/15/92 - 03/15/93) |
| M | = | 2 | (semi-annual) |
| N | = | 56 | (10/12/92 - 09/15/20) |
| R | = | 0.057500 | (5.7500%) |
| RV | = | 100.0000 | |
| Y | = | 0.075000 | (7.5000%) |

**Result:**
| | | |
|---|---|---|
| Price | = | 79.645 |
| Accrued interest | = | 1.87 |

Note: These results are calculated useing M.S.R.B. Rule G–33 in which odd first and/or odd last periods are ignored in calculating price/yield. The accrued interest however, is based on the actual number of days accrued.

## BENCHMARK # 25D

Corporate Bond
| | | |
|---|---|---|
| Settlement date | | 10/12/92 |
| Maturity date | | 09/15/20 |
| Last coupon date | | 06/15/20 |
| Day count basis | | 30/360 |

**Definition of Variables (Formula 14)**
| | | | |
|---|---|---|---|
| A | = | 117 | (06/15/92 - 10/12/92) |
| DLC | = | 90 | (06/15/20 - 09/15/20) |
| DSC | = | 63 | (10/12/92 - 12/15/92) |
| E | = | 180 | (06/15/92 - 12/15/92) |
| M | = | 2 | (semi-annual) |
| N | = | 56 | (10/12/92 - 06/15/20) |
| NLL | = | 180 | (06/15/20 - 12/15/20) |
| R | = | 0.057500 | (5.7500%) |
| RV | = | 100.0000 | |
| Y | = | 0.075000 | (7.5000%) |

**Result:**
| | | |
|---|---|---|
| Price | = | 79.641 |
| Accrued interest | = | 1.87 |

## BENCHMARK # 26A

Treasury Bond
| | |
|---|---|
| Settlement date | 10/12/92 |
| Maturity date | 09/15/20 |
| Last coupon date | 01/15/20 |
| Day count basis | Actual/Actual |

### Definition of Variables (Formula 15)

| | | | |
|---|---|---|---|
| $A$ | = | 89 | (07/15/92 - 10/12/92) |
| $DLC_1$ | = | 182 | (01/15/20 - 07/15/20) |
| $DLC_2$ | = | 62 | (07/15/20 - 09/15/20) |
| $DLQ$ | = | 62 | (07/15/20 - 09/15/20) |
| $DSC$ | = | 95 | (10/12/92 - 01/15/93) |
| $E$ | = | 184 | (07/15/92 - 01/15/93) |
| $LQL$ | = | 184 | (07/15/20 - 01/15/21) |
| $M$ | = | 2 | (semi-annual) |
| $N$ | = | 55 | (10/12/92 - 01/15/20) |
| $NCL$ | = | 2 | (01/15/20 - 09/15/20) |
| $NLL_1$ | = | 182 | (01/15/20 - 07/15/20) |
| $NLL_2$ | = | 184 | (07/15/20 - 01/15/21) |
| $Nql$ | = | 1 | (01/15/20 - 09/15/20) |
| $R$ | = | 0.057500 | (5.7500%) |
| $RV$ | = | 100.0000 | |
| $Y$ | = | 0.075000 | (7.5000%) |

### Result:
| | | |
|---|---|---|
| Price | = | 79.636562 |
| Accrued interest | = | 1.39 |

## BENCHMARK # 26B

Agency Bond
| | |
|---|---|
| Settlement date | 10/12/92 |
| Maturity date | 09/15/20 |
| Last coupon date | 01/15/20 |
| Day count basis | 30/360 |

### Definition of Variables (Formula 15)

| | | | |
|---|---|---|---|
| $A$ | = | 87 | (07/15/92 - 10/12/92) |
| $DLC_1$ | = | 180 | (01/15/20 - 07/15/20) |
| $DLC_2$ | = | 60 | (07/15/20 - 09/15/20) |
| $DLQ$ | = | 60 | (07/15/20 - 09/15/20) |
| $DSC$ | = | 93 | (10/12/92 - 01/15/93) |
| $E$ | = | 180 | (07/15/92 - 01/15/93) |
| $LQL$ | = | 180 | (07/15/20 - 01/15/21) |
| $M$ | = | 2 | (semi-annual) |
| $N$ | = | 55 | (10/12/92 - 01/15/20) |
| $NCL$ | = | 2 | (01/15/20 - 09/15/20) |
| $NLL_1$ | = | 180 | (01/15/20 - 07/15/20) |
| $NLL_2$ | = | 180 | (07/15/20 - 01/15/21) |
| $Nql$ | = | 1 | (01/15/20 - 09/15/20) |
| $R$ | = | 0.057500 | (5.7500%) |
| $RV$ | = | 100.0000 | |
| $Y$ | = | 0.075000 | (7.5000%) |

### Result:
| | | |
|---|---|---|
| Price | = | 79.636079 |
| Accrued interest | = | 1.39 |

## BENCHMARK # 26C

Municipal Bond
| | |
|---|---|
| Settlement date | 10/12/92 |
| Maturity date | 09/15/20 |
| Last coupon date | 03/15/20 |
| Day count basis | 30/360 |

### Definition of Variables (Formula 7)

| | | | |
|---|---|---|---|
| $A$ | = | 27 | (09/15/92 - 10/12/92) |
| $DSC$ | = | 153 | (10/12/92 - 03/15/93) |
| $E$ | = | 180 | (09/15/92 - 03/15/93) |
| $M$ | = | 2 | (semi-annual) |
| $N$ | = | 56 | (10/12/92 - 09/15/20) |
| $R$ | = | 0.057500 | (5.7500%) |
| $RV$ | = | 100.0000 | |
| $Y$ | = | 0.075000 | (7.5000%) |

### Result:
| | | |
|---|---|---|
| Price | = | 79.645 |
| Accrued interest | = | 1.39 |

Note: These results are calculated useing M.S.R.B. Rule G–33 in which odd first and/or odd last periods are ignored in calculating price/yield. The accrued interest however, is based on the actual number of days accrued.

## BENCHMARK # 26D

Corporate Bond
| | |
|---|---|
| Settlement date | 10/12/92 |
| Maturity date | 09/15/20 |
| Last coupon date | 01/15/20 |
| Day count basis | 30/360 |

### Definition of Variables (Formula 15)

| | | | |
|---|---|---|---|
| $A$ | = | 87 | (07/15/92 - 10/12/92) |
| $DLC_1$ | = | 180 | (01/15/20 - 07/15/20) |
| $DLC_2$ | = | 60 | (07/15/20 - 09/15/20) |
| $DLQ$ | = | 60 | (07/15/20 - 09/15/20) |
| $DSC$ | = | 93 | (10/12/92 - 01/15/93) |
| $E$ | = | 180 | (07/15/92 - 01/15/93) |
| $LQL$ | = | 180 | (07/15/20 - 01/15/21) |
| $M$ | = | 2 | (semi-annual) |
| $N$ | = | 55 | (10/12/92 - 01/15/20) |
| $NCL$ | = | 2 | (01/15/20 - 09/15/20) |
| $NLL_1$ | = | 180 | (01/15/20 - 07/15/20) |
| $NLL_2$ | = | 180 | (07/15/20 - 01/15/21) |
| $Nql$ | = | 1 | (01/15/20 - 09/15/20) |
| $R$ | = | 0.057500 | (5.7500%) |
| $RV$ | = | 100.0000 | |
| $Y$ | = | 0.075000 | (7.5000%) |

### Result:
| | | |
|---|---|---|
| Price | = | 79.636 |
| Accrued interest | = | 1.39 |

## BENCHMARK # 27A

Treasury Bond

| | |
|---|---|
| Settlement date | 10/12/92 |
| Maturity date | 06/15/20 |
| Issue/dated date | 05/01/92 |
| First coupon date | 12/31/92 |
| Last coupon date | 12/31/19 |
| Day count basis | Actual/Actual |

### Definition of Variables (Formula 17)

| | | | |
|---|---|---|---|
| A1 | = | 60 | (05/01/92 - 06/30/92) |
| A2 | = | 104 | (06/30/92 - 10/12/92) |
| DFC1 | = | 60 | (05/01/92 - 06/30/92) |
| DFC2 | = | 184 | (06/30/92 - 12/31/92) |
| DLC | = | 167 | (12/31/19 - 06/15/20) |
| DSC | = | 80 | (10/12/92 - 12/31/92) |
| E | = | 184 | (06/30/92 - 12/31/92) |
| M | = | 2 | (semi-annual) |
| N | = | 54 | (12/31/92 - 12/31/19) |
| NCF | = | 2 | (05/01/92 - 12/31/92) |
| $NLF_1$ | = | 182 | (12/31/91 - 06/30/92) |
| $NLF_2$ | = | 184 | (06/30/92 - 12/31/92) |
| Nqf | = | 0 | (10/12/92 - 12/31/92) |
| R | = | 0.057500 | (5.7500%) |
| RV | = | 100.0000 | |
| Y | = | 0.065000 | (6.5000%) |

### Result:

| | | |
|---|---|---|
| Price | = | 90.402804 |
| Accrued interest | = | 2.57 |

## BENCHMARK # 27B

Agency Bond

| | |
|---|---|
| Settlement date | 10/12/92 |
| Maturity date | 06/15/20 |
| Issue/dated date | 05/01/92 |
| First coupon date | 12/31/92 |
| Last coupon date | 12/31/19 |
| Day count basis | 30/360 |

### Definition of Variables (Formula 17)

| | | | |
|---|---|---|---|
| A1 | = | 59 | (05/01/92 - 06/30/92) |
| A2 | = | 102 | (06/30/92 - 10/12/92) |
| DFC1 | = | 59 | (05/01/92 - 06/30/92) |
| DFC2 | = | 180 | (06/30/92 - 12/31/92) |
| DLC | = | 165 | (12/31/19 - 06/15/20) |
| DSC | = | 78 | (10/12/92 - 12/31/92) |
| E | = | 180 | (06/30/92 - 12/31/92) |
| M | = | 2 | (semi-annual) |
| N | = | 54 | (12/31/92 - 12/31/19) |
| NCF | = | 2 | (05/01/92 - 12/31/92) |
| $NLF_1$ | = | 180 | (12/31/91 - 06/30/92) |
| $NLF_2$ | = | 180 | (06/30/92 - 12/31/92) |
| Nqf | = | 0 | (10/12/92 - 12/31/92) |
| R | = | 0.057500 | (5.7500%) |
| RV | = | 100.0000 | |
| Y | = | 0.065000 | (6.5000%) |

### Result:

| | | |
|---|---|---|
| Price | = | 90.403123 |
| Accrued interest | = | 2.57 |

## BENCHMARK # 27C

Municipal Bond

| | |
|---|---|
| Settlement date | 10/12/92 |
| Maturity date | 06/15/20 |
| Issue/dated date | 05/01/92 |
| First coupon date | 12/31/92 |
| Last coupon date | 12/15/19 |
| Day count basis | 30/360 |

**Definition of Variables (Formula 7)**

| | | | |
|---|---|---|---|
| A | = | 117 | (06/15/92 - 10/12/92) |
| DSC | = | 63 | (10/12/92 - 12/15/92) |
| E | = | 180 | (06/15/92 - 12/15/92) |
| M | = | 2 | (semi-annual) |
| N | = | 56 | (10/12/92 - 06/15/20) |
| R | = | 0.057500 | (5.7500%) |
| RV | = | 100.0000 | |
| Y | = | 0.065000 | (6.5000%) |

**Result:**

| | | |
|---|---|---|
| Price | = | 90.415 |
| Accrued interest | = | 2.57 |

Note: These results are calculated useing M.S.R.B. Rule G–33 in which odd first and/or odd last periods are ignored in calculating price/yield. The accrued interest however, is based on the actual number of days accrued.

## BENCHMARK # 27D

Corporate Bond

| | |
|---|---|
| Settlement date | 10/12/92 |
| Maturity date | 06/15/20 |
| Issue/dated date | 05/01/92 |
| First coupon date | 12/31/92 |
| Last coupon date | 12/31/19 |
| Day count basis | 30/360 |

**Definition of Variables (Formula 17)**

| | | | |
|---|---|---|---|
| A1 | = | 59 | (05/01/92 - 06/30/92) |
| A2 | = | 102 | (06/30/92 - 10/12/92) |
| DFC1 | = | 59 | (05/01/92 - 06/30/92) |
| DFC2 | = | 180 | (06/30/92 - 12/31/92) |
| DLC | = | 165 | (12/31/19 - 06/15/20) |
| DSC | = | 78 | (10/12/92 - 12/31/92) |
| E | = | 180 | (06/30/92 - 12/31/92) |
| M | = | 2 | (semi-annual) |
| N | = | 54 | (12/31/92 - 12/31/19) |
| NCF | = | 2 | (05/01/92 - 12/31/92) |
| $NLF_1$ | = | 180 | (12/31/91 - 06/30/92) |
| $NLF_2$ | = | 180 | (06/30/92 - 12/31/92) |
| Nqf | = | 0 | (10/12/92 - 12/31/92) |
| R | = | 0.057500 | (5.7500%) |
| RV | = | 100.0000 | |
| Y | = | 0.065000 | (6.5000%) |

**Result:**

| | | |
|---|---|---|
| Price | = | 90.403 |
| Accrued interest | = | 2.57 |

## BENCHMARK # 28A

Treasury Bond
| | |
|---|---|
| Settlement date | 10/12/92 |
| Maturity date | 09/15/20 |
| Issue/dated date | 08/01/92 |
| First coupon date | 12/31/92 |
| Last coupon date | 12/31/19 |
| Day count basis | Actual/Actual |

### Definition of Variables (Formula 18)

| | | | |
|---|---|---|---|
| $A$ | = | 72 | (08/01/92 - 10/12/92) |
| $DFC$ | = | 152 | (08/01/92 - 12/31/92) |
| $DLC_1$ | = | 182 | (12/31/19 - 06/30/20) |
| $DLC_2$ | = | 77 | (06/30/20 - 09/15/20) |
| $DLQ$ | = | 77 | (06/30/20 - 09/15/20) |
| $DSC$ | = | 80 | (10/12/92 - 12/31/92) |
| $E$ | = | 184 | (06/30/92 - 12/31/92) |
| $LQL$ | = | 184 | (06/30/20 - 12/31/20) |
| $M$ | = | 2 | (semi-annual) |
| $N$ | = | 55 | (10/12/92 - 12/31/19) |
| $NCL$ | = | 2 | (12/31/19 - 09/15/20) |
| $NLL_1$ | = | 182 | (12/31/19 - 06/30/20) |
| $NLL_2$ | = | 184 | (06/30/20 - 12/31/20) |
| $Nql$ | = | 1 | (12/31/19 - 09/15/20) |
| $R$ | = | 0.057500 | (5.7500%) |
| $RV$ | = | 100.0000 | |
| $Y$ | = | 0.065000 | (6.5000%) |

### Result:
| | | |
|---|---|---|
| Price | = | 90.386498 |
| Accrued interest | = | 1.13 |

## BENCHMARK # 28B

Agency Bond
| | |
|---|---|
| Settlement date | 10/12/92 |
| Maturity date | 09/15/20 |
| Issue/dated date | 08/01/92 |
| First coupon date | 12/31/92 |
| Last coupon date | 12/31/19 |
| Day count basis | 30/360 |

### Definition of Variables (Formula 18)

| | | | |
|---|---|---|---|
| $A$ | = | 71 | (08/01/92 - 10/12/92) |
| $DFC$ | = | 150 | (08/01/92 - 12/31/92) |
| $DLC_1$ | = | 180 | (12/31/19 - 06/30/20) |
| $DLC_2$ | = | 75 | (06/30/20 - 09/15/20) |
| $DLQ$ | = | 75 | (06/30/20 - 09/15/20) |
| $DSC$ | = | 79 | (10/12/92 - 12/31/92) |
| $E$ | = | 180 | (06/30/92 - 12/31/92) |
| $LQL$ | = | 180 | (06/30/20 - 12/31/20) |
| $M$ | = | 2 | (semi-annual) |
| $N$ | = | 55 | (10/12/92 - 12/31/19) |
| $NCL$ | = | 2 | (12/31/19 - 09/15/20) |
| $NLL_1$ | = | 180 | (12/31/19 - 06/30/20) |
| $NLL_2$ | = | 180 | (06/30/20 - 12/31/20) |
| $Nql$ | = | 1 | (12/31/19 - 09/15/20) |
| $R$ | = | 0.057500 | (5.7500%) |
| $RV$ | = | 100.0000 | |
| $Y$ | = | 0.065000 | (6.5000%) |

### Result:
| | | |
|---|---|---|
| Price | = | 90.386581 |
| Accrued interest | = | 1.13 |

## BENCHMARK # 28c

Municipal Bond

| | |
|---|---|
| Settlement date | 10/12/92 |
| Maturity date | 09/15/20 |
| Issue/dated date | 08/01/92 |
| First coupon date | 12/31/92 |
| Last coupon date | 03/15/20 |
| Day count basis | 30/360 |

**Definition of Variables (Formula 7)**

| | | | |
|---|---|---|---|
| A | = | 27 | (09/15/92 - 10/12/92) |
| DSC | = | 153 | (10/12/92 - 03/15/93) |
| E | = | 180 | (09/15/92 - 03/15/93) |
| M | = | 2 | (semi-annual) |
| N | = | 56 | (10/12/92 - 09/15/20) |
| R | = | 0.057500 | (5.7500%) |
| RV | = | 100.0000 | |
| Y | = | 0.065000 | (6.5000%) |

**Result:**

| | | |
|---|---|---|
| Price | = | 90.389 |
| Accrued interest | = | 1.13 |

Note: These results are calculated useing M.S.R.B. Rule G–33 in which odd first and/or odd last periods are ignored in calculating price/yield. The accrued interest however, is based on the actual number of days accrued.

## BENCHMARK # 28d

Corporate Bond

| | |
|---|---|
| Settlement date | 10/12/92 |
| Maturity date | 09/15/20 |
| Issue/dated date | 08/01/92 |
| First coupon date | 12/31/92 |
| Last coupon date | 12/31/19 |
| Day count basis | 30/360 |

**Definition of Variables (Formula 18)**

| | | | |
|---|---|---|---|
| A | = | 71 | (08/01/92 - 10/12/92) |
| DFC | = | 150 | (08/01/92 - 12/31/92) |
| $DLC_1$ | = | 180 | (12/31/19 - 06/30/20) |
| $DLC_2$ | = | 75 | (06/30/20 - 09/15/20) |
| DLQ | = | 75 | (06/30/20 - 09/15/20) |
| DSC | = | 79 | (10/12/92 - 12/31/92) |
| E | = | 180 | (06/30/92 - 12/31/92) |
| LQL | = | 180 | (06/30/20 - 12/31/20) |
| M | = | 2 | (semi-annual) |
| N | = | 55 | (10/12/92 - 12/31/19) |
| NCL | = | 2 | (12/31/19 - 09/15/20) |
| $NLL_1$ | = | 180 | (12/31/19 - 06/30/20) |
| $NLL_2$ | = | 180 | (06/30/20 - 12/31/20) |
| Nql | = | 1 | (12/31/19 - 09/15/20) |
| R | = | 0.057500 | (5.7500%) |
| RV | = | 100.0000 | |
| Y | = | 0.065000 | (6.5000%) |

**Result:**

| | | |
|---|---|---|
| Price | = | 90.386 |
| Accrued interest | = | 1.13 |

## BENCHMARK # 29A

Treasury Bond
| | |
|---|---|
| Settlement date | 10/12/92 |
| Maturity date | 09/15/20 |
| Issue/dated date | 03/01/92 |
| First coupon date | 12/31/92 |
| Last coupon date | 12/31/19 |
| Day count basis | Actual/Actual |

**Definition of Variables (Formula 19)**

| | | | |
|---|---|---|---|
| A1 | = | 121 | (03/01/92 - 06/30/92) |
| A2 | = | 104 | (06/30/92 - 10/12/92) |
| DFC1 | = | 121 | (03/01/92 - 06/30/92) |
| DFC2 | = | 184 | (06/30/92 - 12/31/92) |
| $DLC_1$ | = | 182 | (12/31/19 - 06/30/20) |
| $DLC_2$ | = | 77 | (06/30/20 - 09/15/20) |
| DLQ | = | 77 | (06/30/20 - 09/15/20) |
| DSC | = | 80 | (10/12/92 - 12/31/92) |
| E | = | 184 | (06/30/92 - 12/31/92) |
| LQL | = | 184 | (06/30/20 - 12/31/20) |
| M | = | 2 | (semi-annual) |
| N | = | 54 | (12/31/92 - 12/31/19) |
| NCF | = | 2 | (03/01/92 - 12/31/92) |
| NCL | = | 2 | (12/31/19 - 09/15/20) |
| $NLF_1$ | = | 182 | (12/31/91 - 06/30/92) |
| $NLF_2$ | = | 184 | (06/30/92 - 12/31/92) |
| $NLL_1$ | = | 182 | (12/31/19 - 06/30/20) |
| $NLL_2$ | = | 184 | (06/30/20 - 12/31/20) |
| Nqf | = | 0 | (10/12/92 - 12/31/92) |
| Nql | = | 1 | (12/31/19 - 09/15/20) |
| R | = | 0.057500 | (5.7500%) |
| RV | = | 100.0000 | |
| Y | = | 0.065000 | (6.5000%) |

**Result:**
| | | |
|---|---|---|
| Price | = | 90.353198 |
| Accrued interest | = | 3.54 |

## BENCHMARK # 29B

Agency Bond
| | |
|---|---|
| Settlement date | 10/12/92 |
| Maturity date | 09/15/20 |
| Issue/dated date | 03/01/92 |
| First coupon date | 12/31/92 |
| Last coupon date | 12/31/19 |
| Day count basis | 30/360 |

**Definition of Variables (Formula 19)**

| | | | |
|---|---|---|---|
| A1 | = | 119 | (03/01/92 - 06/30/92) |
| A2 | = | 102 | (06/30/92 - 10/12/92) |
| DFC1 | = | 119 | (03/01/92 - 06/30/92) |
| DFC2 | = | 180 | (06/30/92 - 12/31/92) |
| $DLC_1$ | = | 180 | (12/31/19 - 06/30/20) |
| $DLC_2$ | = | 75 | (06/30/20 - 09/15/20) |
| DLQ | = | 75 | (06/30/20 - 09/15/20) |
| DSC | = | 78 | (10/12/92 - 12/31/92) |
| E | = | 180 | (06/30/92 - 12/31/92) |
| LQL | = | 180 | (06/30/20 - 12/31/20) |
| M | = | 2 | (semi-annual) |
| N | = | 54 | (12/31/92 - 12/31/19) |
| NCF | = | 2 | (03/01/92 - 12/31/92) |
| NCL | = | 2 | (12/31/19 - 09/15/20) |
| $NLF_1$ | = | 180 | (12/31/91 - 06/30/92) |
| $NLF_2$ | = | 180 | (06/30/92 - 12/31/92) |
| $NLL_1$ | = | 180 | (12/31/19 - 06/30/20) |
| $NLL_2$ | = | 180 | (06/30/20 - 12/31/20) |
| Nqf | = | 0 | (10/12/92 - 12/31/92) |
| Nql | = | 1 | (12/31/19 - 09/15/20) |
| R | = | 0.057500 | (5.7500%) |
| RV | = | 100.0000 | |
| Y | = | 0.065000 | (6.5000%) |

**Result:**
| | | |
|---|---|---|
| Price | = | 90.353605 |
| Accrued interest | = | 3.53 |

## BENCHMARK # 29c

Municipal Bond

| | |
|---|---|
| Settlement date | 10/12/92 |
| Maturity date | 09/15/20 |
| Issue/dated date | 03/01/92 |
| First coupon date | 12/31/92 |
| Last coupon date | 03/15/20 |
| Day count basis | 30/360 |

### Definition of Variables (Formula 7)

| | | | |
|---|---|---|---|
| A | = | 27 | (09/15/92 - 10/12/92) |
| DSC | = | 153 | (10/12/92 - 03/15/93) |
| E | = | 180 | (09/15/92 - 03/15/93) |
| M | = | 2 | (semi-annual) |
| N | = | 56 | (10/12/92 - 09/15/20) |
| R | = | 0.057500 | (5.7500%) |
| RV | = | 100.0000 | |
| Y | = | 0.065000 | (6.5000%) |

### Result:

| | | |
|---|---|---|
| Price | = | 90.389 |
| Accrued interest | = | 3.53 |

Note: These results are calculated useing M.S.R.B. Rule G–33 in which odd first and/or odd last periods are ignored in calculating price/yield. The accrued interest however, is based on the actual number of days accrued.

## BENCHMARK # 29d

Corporate Bond

| | |
|---|---|
| Settlement date | 10/12/92 |
| Maturity date | 09/15/20 |
| Issue/dated date | 03/01/92 |
| First coupon date | 12/31/92 |
| Last coupon date | 12/31/19 |
| Day count basis | 30/360 |

### Definition of Variables (Formula 19)

| | | | |
|---|---|---|---|
| A1 | = | 119 | (03/01/92 - 06/30/92) |
| A2 | = | 102 | (06/30/92 - 10/12/92) |
| DFC1 | = | 119 | (03/01/92 - 06/30/92) |
| DFC2 | = | 180 | (06/30/92 - 12/31/92) |
| $DLC_1$ | = | 180 | (12/31/19 - 06/30/20) |
| $DLC_2$ | = | 75 | (06/30/20 - 09/15/20) |
| DLQ | = | 75 | (06/30/20 - 09/15/20) |
| DSC | = | 78 | (10/12/92 - 12/31/92) |
| E | = | 180 | (06/30/92 - 12/31/92) |
| LQL | = | 180 | (06/30/20 - 12/31/20) |
| M | = | 2 | (semi-annual) |
| N | = | 54 | (12/31/92 - 12/31/19) |
| NCF | = | 2 | (03/01/92 - 12/31/92) |
| NCL | = | 2 | (12/31/19 - 09/15/20) |
| $NLF_1$ | = | 180 | (12/31/91 - 06/30/92) |
| $NLF_2$ | = | 180 | (06/30/92 - 12/31/92) |
| $NLL_1$ | = | 180 | (12/31/19 - 06/30/20) |
| $NLL_2$ | = | 180 | (06/30/20 - 12/31/20) |
| Nqf | = | 0 | (10/12/92 - 12/31/92) |
| Nql | = | 1 | (12/31/19 - 09/15/20) |
| R | = | 0.057500 | (5.7500%) |
| RV | = | 100.0000 | |
| Y | = | 0.065000 | (6.5000%) |

### Result:

| | | |
|---|---|---|
| Price | = | 90.353 |
| Accrued interest | = | 3.53 |

## BENCHMARK # 30A

Treasury Bond (Zero coupon)
Settlement date          06/24/93
Maturity date           11/01/93
Day count basis         Actual/Actual

**Definition of Variables (Formula 21)**
DSR = 130       (06/24/93 - 11/01/93)
  E = 184       (05/01/93 - 11/01/93)
  M = 2         (semi-annual)
 RV = 100.0000
  Y = 0.040000  (4.0000%)

**Result:**
Price             =   98.606645
Accrued interest  =   0.00

## BENCHMARK # 30B

Agency Bond (Zero coupon)
Settlement date          06/24/93
Maturity date           11/01/93
Day count basis         30/360

**Definition of Variables (Formula 21)**
DSR = 127       (06/24/93 - 11/01/93)
  E = 180       (05/01/93 - 11/01/93)
  M = 2         (semi-annual)
 RV = 100.0000
  Y = 0.040000  (4.0000%)

**Result:**
Price             =   98.608524
Accrued interest  =   0.00

## BENCHMARK # 30C

Municipal Bond (Zero coupon)
Settlement date          06/24/93
Maturity date           11/01/93
Day count basis         30/360

**Definition of Variables (Formula 21)**
DSR = 127       (06/24/93 - 11/01/93)
  E = 180       (05/01/93 - 11/01/93)
  M = 2         (semi-annual)
 RV = 100.0000
  Y = 0.040000  (4.0000%)

**Result:**
Price             =   98.608
Accrued interest  =   0.00

## BENCHMARK # 30D

Corporate Bond (Zero coupon)
Settlement date          06/24/93
Maturity date           11/01/93
Day count basis         30/360

**Definition of Variables (Formula 21)**
DSR = 127       (06/24/93 - 11/01/93)
  E = 180       (05/01/93 - 11/01/93)
  M = 2         (semi-annual)
 RV = 100.0000
  Y = 0.040000  (4.0000%)

**Result:**
Price             =   98.608
Accrued interest  =   0.00

## BENCHMARK # 31A

Treasury Bond (Zero coupon)
| | |
|---|---|
| Settlement date | 06/24/93 |
| Maturity date | 11/01/93 |
| Day count basis | Actual/Actual |

**Definition of Variables (Formula 20)**

| | | | |
|---|---|---|---|
| DSR | = | 130 | (06/24/93 - 11/01/93) |
| E | = | 184 | (05/01/93 - 11/01/93) |
| M | = | 2 | (semi-annual) |
| P | = | 95.0000 | ($95.0000) |
| RV | = | 100.0000 | |

**Result:**

| | | |
|---|---|---|
| Yield | = | 14.898785 |
| Accrued interest | = | 0.00 |

## BENCHMARK # 31B

Agency Bond (Zero coupon)
| | |
|---|---|
| Settlement date | 06/24/93 |
| Maturity date | 11/01/93 |
| Day count basis | 30/360 |

**Definition of Variables (Formula 20)**

| | | | |
|---|---|---|---|
| DSR | = | 127 | (06/24/93 - 11/01/93) |
| E | = | 180 | (05/01/93 - 11/01/93) |
| M | = | 2 | (semi-annual) |
| P | = | 95.0000 | ($95.0000) |
| RV | = | 100.0000 | |

**Result:**

| | | |
|---|---|---|
| Yield | = | 14.919188 |
| Accrued interest | = | 0.00 |

## BENCHMARK # 31C

Municipal Bond (Zero coupon)
| | |
|---|---|
| Settlement date | 06/24/93 |
| Maturity date | 11/01/93 |
| Day count basis | 30/360 |

**Definition of Variables (Formula 20)**

| | | | |
|---|---|---|---|
| DSR | = | 127 | (06/24/93 - 11/01/93) |
| E | = | 180 | (05/01/93 - 11/01/93) |
| M | = | 2 | (semi-annual) |
| P | = | 95.0000 | ($95.0000) |
| RV | = | 100.0000 | |

**Result:**

| | | |
|---|---|---|
| Yield | = | 14.919 |
| Accrued interest | = | 0.00 |

## BENCHMARK # 31D

Corporate Bond (Zero coupon)
| | |
|---|---|
| Settlement date | 06/24/93 |
| Maturity date | 11/01/93 |
| Day count basis | 30/360 |

**Definition of Variables (Formula 20)**

| | | | |
|---|---|---|---|
| DSR | = | 127 | (06/24/93 - 11/01/93) |
| E | = | 180 | (05/01/93 - 11/01/93) |
| M | = | 2 | (semi-annual) |
| P | = | 95.0000 | ($95.0000) |
| RV | = | 100.0000 | |

**Result:**

| | | |
|---|---|---|
| Yield | = | 14.919 |
| Accrued interest | = | 0.00 |

## BENCHMARK # 32A

Treasury Bond (Zero coupon)
Settlement date          06/24/93
Maturity date            01/15/24
Day count basis          Actual/Actual

**Definition of Variables (Formula 23)**

| | | | |
|---|---|---|---|
| DSC | = | 21 | (06/24/93 - 07/15/93) |
| E | = | 181 | (01/15/93 - 07/15/93) |
| M | = | 2 | (semi-annual) |
| Nq | = | 62 | (06/24/93 - 01/15/24) |
| RV | = | 100.0000 | |
| Y | = | 0.100000 | (10.0000%) |

**Result:**

Price             =    5.069841
Accrued interest  =    0.00

## BENCHMARK # 32B

Agency Bond (Zero coupon)
Settlement date          06/24/93
Maturity date            01/15/24
Day count basis          30/360

**Definition of Variables (Formula 23)**

| | | | |
|---|---|---|---|
| DSC | = | 21 | (06/24/93 - 07/15/93) |
| E | = | 180 | (01/15/93 - 07/15/93) |
| M | = | 2 | (semi-annual) |
| Nq | = | 62 | (06/24/93 - 01/15/24) |
| RV | = | 100.0000 | |
| Y | = | 0.100000 | (10.0000%) |

**Result:**

Price             =    5.069681
Accrued interest  =    0.00

## BENCHMARK # 32C

Municipal Bond (Zero coupon)
Settlement date          06/24/93
Maturity date            01/15/24
Day count basis          30/360

**Definition of Variables (Formula 23)**

| | | | |
|---|---|---|---|
| DSC | = | 21 | (06/24/93 - 07/15/93) |
| E | = | 180 | (01/15/93 - 07/15/93) |
| M | = | 2 | (semi-annual) |
| Nq | = | 62 | (06/24/93 - 01/15/24) |
| RV | = | 100.0000 | |
| Y | = | 0.100000 | (10.0000%) |

**Result:**

Price             =    5.069
Accrued interest  =    0.00

## BENCHMARK # 32D

Corporate Bond (Zero coupon)
Settlement date          06/24/93
Maturity date            01/15/24
Day count basis          30/360

**Definition of Variables (Formula 23)**

| | | | |
|---|---|---|---|
| DSC | = | 21 | (06/24/93 - 07/15/93) |
| E | = | 180 | (01/15/93 - 07/15/93) |
| M | = | 2 | (semi-annual) |
| Nq | = | 62 | (06/24/93 - 01/15/24) |
| RV | = | 100.0000 | |
| Y | = | 0.100000 | (10.0000%) |

**Result:**

Price             =    5.069
Accrued interest  =    0.00

## BENCHMARK # 33A

Treasury Bond (Zero coupon)
Settlement date            06/24/93
Maturity date              01/15/24
Day count basis            Actual/Actual

**Definition of Variables (Formula 22)**

| | | | |
|---|---|---|---|
| DSC | = | 21 | (06/24/93 - 07/15/93) |
| E | = | 181 | (01/15/93 - 07/15/93) |
| M | = | 2 | (semi-annual) |
| Nq | = | 62 | (06/24/93 - 01/15/24) |
| P | = | 9.0000 | ($9.0000 ) |
| RV | = | 100.0000 | |

**Result:**

Yield            =      8.037208
Accrued interest   =      0.00

## BENCHMARK # 33B

Agency Bond (Zero coupon)
Settlement date            06/24/93
Maturity date              01/15/24
Day count basis            30/360

**Definition of Variables (Formula 22)**

| | | | |
|---|---|---|---|
| DSC | = | 21 | (06/24/93 - 07/15/93) |
| E | = | 180 | (01/15/93 - 07/15/93) |
| M | = | 2 | (semi-annual) |
| Nq | = | 62 | (06/24/93 - 01/15/24) |
| P | = | 9.0000 | ($9.0000 ) |
| RV | = | 100.0000 | |

**Result:**

Yield            =      8.037121
Accrued interest   =      0.00

## BENCHMARK # 33C

Municipal Bond (Zero coupon)
Settlement date            06/24/93
Maturity date              01/15/24
Day count basis            30/360

**Definition of Variables (Formula 22)**

| | | | |
|---|---|---|---|
| DSC | = | 21 | (06/24/93 - 07/15/93) |
| E | = | 180 | (01/15/93 - 07/15/93) |
| M | = | 2 | (semi-annual) |
| Nq | = | 62 | (06/24/93 - 01/15/24) |
| P | = | 9.0000 | ($9.0000 ) |
| RV | = | 100.0000 | |

**Result:**

Yield            =      8.037
Accrued interest   =      0.00

## BENCHMARK # 33D

Corporate Bond (Zero coupon)
Settlement date            06/24/93
Maturity date              01/15/24
Day count basis            30/360

**Definition of Variables (Formula 22)**

| | | | |
|---|---|---|---|
| DSC | = | 21 | (06/24/93 - 07/15/93) |
| E | = | 180 | (01/15/93 - 07/15/93) |
| M | = | 2 | (semi-annual) |
| Nq | = | 62 | (06/24/93 - 01/15/24) |
| P | = | 9.0000 | ($9.0000 ) |
| RV | = | 100.0000 | |

**Result:**

Yield            =      8.037
Accrued interest   =      0.00

## BENCHMARK # 34A

Municipal Note
Settlement date          06/05/93
Maturity date            09/01/93
Issue/dated date         01/01/93
Day count basis          30/360

**Definition of Variables (Formula 4)**

| | | | |
|---|---|---|---|
| A | = | 154 | (01/01/93 - 06/05/93) |
| B | = | 360 | (30/360) |
| DIM | = | 240 | (01/01/93 - 09/01/93) |
| DSM | = | 86 | (06/05/93 - 09/01/93) |
| R | = | 0.063750 | (6.3750%) |
| RV | = | 100.0000 | |
| Y | = | 0.080000 | (8.0000%) |

**Result:**

Price            =    99.567
Accrued interest =    2.73

## BENCHMARK # 34B

Municipal Note
Settlement date          06/05/93
Maturity date            09/01/93
Issue/dated date         01/01/93
Day count basis          Actual/360

**Definition of Variables (Formula 4)**

| | | | |
|---|---|---|---|
| A | = | 155 | (01/01/93 - 06/05/93) |
| B | = | 360 | (Act/360) |
| DIM | = | 243 | (01/01/93 - 09/01/93) |
| DSM | = | 88 | (06/05/93 - 09/01/93) |
| R | = | 0.063750 | (6.3750%) |
| RV | = | 100.0000 | |
| Y | = | 0.080000 | (8.0000%) |

**Result:**

Price            =    99.557
Accrued interest =    2.74

## BENCHMARK # 34C

Municipal Note
Settlement date          06/05/93
Maturity date            09/01/93
Issue/dated date         01/01/93
Day count basis          Actual/365

**Definition of Variables (Formula 4)**

| | | | |
|---|---|---|---|
| A | = | 155 | (01/01/93 - 06/05/93) |
| B | = | 365 | (Act/365) |
| DIM | = | 243 | (01/01/93 - 09/01/93) |
| DSM | = | 88 | (06/05/93 - 09/01/93) |
| R | = | 0.063750 | (6.3750%) |
| RV | = | 100.0000 | |
| Y | = | 0.080000 | (8.0000%) |

**Result:**

Price            =    99.564
Accrued interest =    2.71

## BENCHMARK # 35A

Municipal Note
Settlement date          06/05/93
Maturity date            09/01/93
Issue/dated date         01/01/93
Day count basis          30/360

**Definition of Variables (Formula 3)**

| | | | |
|---|---|---|---|
| A | = | 154 | (01/01/93 - 06/05/93) |
| B | = | 360 | (30/360) |
| DIM | = | 240 | (01/01/93 - 09/01/93) |
| DSM | = | 86 | (06/05/93 - 09/01/93) |
| P | = | 98.0000 | ($98.0000) |
| R | = | 0.063750 | (6.3750%) |
| RV | = | 100.0000 | |

**Result:**

Yield            =    14.641
Accrued interest =     2.73

## BENCHMARK # 35B

Municipal Note
Settlement date          06/05/93
Maturity date            09/01/93
Issue/dated date         01/01/93
Day count basis          Actual/360

**Definition of Variables (Formula 3)**

| | | | |
|---|---|---|---|
| A | = | 155 | (01/01/93 - 06/05/93) |
| B | = | 360 | (Act/360) |
| DIM | = | 243 | (01/01/93 - 09/01/93) |
| DSM | = | 88 | (06/05/93 - 09/01/93) |
| P | = | 98.0000 | ($98.0000) |
| R | = | 0.063750 | (6.3750%) |
| RV | = | 100.0000 | |

**Result:**

Yield            =    14.449
Accrued interest =     2.74

## BENCHMARK # 35C

Municipal Note
Settlement date          06/05/93
Maturity date            09/01/93
Issue/dated date         01/01/93
Day count basis          Actual/365

**Definition of Variables (Formula 3)**

| | | | |
|---|---|---|---|
| A | = | 155 | (01/01/93 - 06/05/93) |
| B | = | 365 | (Act/365) |
| DIM | = | 243 | (01/01/93 - 09/01/93) |
| DSM | = | 88 | (06/05/93 - 09/01/93) |
| P | = | 98.0000 | ($98.0000) |
| R | = | 0.063750 | (6.3750%) |
| RV | = | 100.0000 | |

**Result:**

Yield            =    14.567
Accrued interest =     2.71

## Benchmark # 36a

Treasury Bill
Settlement date      01/01/92
Maturity date      01/01/93
Day count basis      Actual/360

**Definition of Variables (Formula 1)**

| | | | |
|---|---|---|---|
| B | = | 360 | (Act/360) |
| DSM | = | 366 | (01/01/92 - 01/01/93) |
| P | = | 98.0000 | ($98.0000) |
| RV | = | 100.0000 | |

**Result:**
Yield      =      2.007360

## Benchmark # 36b

Treasury Bill
Settlement date      01/01/92
Maturity date      07/01/92
Day count basis      Actual/360

**Definition of Variables (Formula 1)**

| | | | |
|---|---|---|---|
| B | = | 360 | (Act/360) |
| DSM | = | 182 | (01/01/92 - 07/01/92) |
| P | = | 98.0000 | ($98.0000) |
| RV | = | 100.0000 | |

**Result:**
Yield      =      4.036780

## Benchmark # 37a

Treasury Bill
Settlement date      01/01/92
Maturity date      01/01/93
Day count basis      Actual/360

**Definition of Variables (Formula 2)**

| | | | |
|---|---|---|---|
| B | = | 360 | (Act/360) |
| DR | = | 0.038750 | (3.8750%) |
| DSM | = | 366 | (01/01/92 - 01/01/93) |
| RV | = | 100.0000 | |

**Result:**
Price      =      96.0604167

## Benchmark # 37b

Treasury Bill
Settlement date      01/01/92
Maturity date      07/01/92
Day count basis      Actual/360

**Definition of Variables (Formula 2)**

| | | | |
|---|---|---|---|
| B | = | 360 | (Act/360) |
| DR | = | 0.038750 | (3.8750%) |
| DSM | = | 182 | (01/01/92 - 07/01/92) |
| RV | = | 100.0000 | |

**Result:**
Price      =      98.0409722

## BENCHMARK # 38A

Treasury Bill
Settlement date  01/01/93
Maturity date   01/01/94
Day count basis  Actual/360

**Definition of Variables (Formula 1)**

| | | | |
|---|---|---|---|
| B | = | 360 | (Act/360) |
| DSM | = | 365 | (01/01/93 - 01/01/94) |
| P | = | 99.0000 | ($99.0000) |
| RV | = | 100.0000 | |

**Result:**
Yield    =  0.996264

## BENCHMARK # 38B

Treasury Bill
Settlement date  01/01/93
Maturity date   07/01/93
Day count basis  Actual/360

**Definition of Variables (Formula 1)**

| | | | |
|---|---|---|---|
| B | = | 360 | (Act/360) |
| DSM | = | 181 | (01/01/93 - 07/01/93) |
| P | = | 99.0000 | ($99.0000) |
| RV | = | 100.0000 | |

**Result:**
Yield    =  2.009041

## BENCHMARK # 39A

Treasury Bill
Settlement date  01/01/93
Maturity date   01/01/94
Day count basis  Actual/360

**Definition of Variables (Formula 2)**

| | | | |
|---|---|---|---|
| B | = | 360 | (Act/360) |
| DR | = | 0.068750 | (6.8750%) |
| DSM | = | 365 | (01/01/93 - 01/01/94) |
| RV | = | 100.0000 | |

**Result:**
Price    =  93.0295139

## BENCHMARK # 39B

Treasury Bill
Settlement date  01/01/93
Maturity date   07/01/93
Day count basis  Actual/360

**Definition of Variables (Formula 2)**

| | | | |
|---|---|---|---|
| B | = | 360 | (Act/360) |
| DR | = | 0.068750 | (6.8750%) |
| DSM | = | 181 | (01/01/93 - 07/01/93) |
| RV | = | 100.0000 | |

**Result:**
Price    =  96.5434028